Singapore MATH

LEVEL **4**

Appropriate for Students in GRADE **5**

W9-BKM-956

70 Must-Know WORD PROBLEMS

Frank Schaffer Publications®

Columbus, Ohio

Frank Schaffer Publications®

This edition published in 2009 in the United States of America by Frank Schaffer Publications. Frank Schaffer Publications is an imprint of School Specialty Publishing.

Send all inquiries to:
Frank Schaffer Publications
8720 Orion Place
Columbus, Ohio 43240-2111

70 Must-Know Word Problems Level 4

ISBN 0-7682-4014-X

1 2 3 4 5 6 7 8 9 10 GLO 12 11 10 09

INTRODUCTION TO SINGAPORE MATH

At an elementary level, some simple mathematical skills can help students understand mathematical principles. These skills are the counting-on, counting-back, and crossing-out methods. Note that these methods are most useful when the numbers are small.

1. The Counting-On Method

Used for addition of two numbers. Count on in 1s with the help of a picture or number line.

$$7 + 4 = \mathbf{11}$$

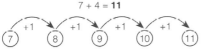

2. The Counting-Back Method

Used for subtraction of two numbers. Count back in 1s with the help of a picture or number line.

$$16 - 3 = \mathbf{13}$$

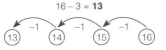

3. The Crossing-Out Method

Used for subtraction of two numbers. Cross out the number of items to be taken away. Count the remaining ones to find the answer.

$$20 - 12 = \mathbf{8}$$

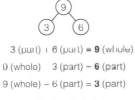

A **number bond** shows the relationship in a simple addition or subtraction problem. The number bond is based on the concept "part-part-whole." This concept is useful in teaching simple addition and subtraction to young children.

To find a whole, students must add the two parts.
To find a part, students must subtract the other part from the whole.

The different types of number bonds are illustrated below.

1. Number Bond (single digits)

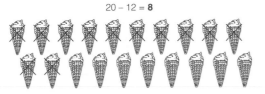

3 (part) + 6 (part) = **9** (whole)

9 (whole) – 3 (part) = **6** (part)

9 (whole) – 6 (part) = **3** (part)

2. Addition Number Bond (single digits)

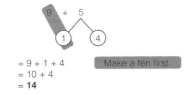

= 9 + 1 + 4   Make a ten first.
= 10 + 4
= **14**

3. Addition Number Bond (double and single digits)

= 2 + 5 + 10   Regroup 15 into 5 and 10.
= 7 + 10
= **17**

4. Subtraction Number Bond (double and single digits)

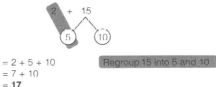

10 – 7 = 3
3 + 2 = **5**

5. Subtraction Number Bond (double digits)

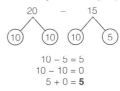

10 – 5 = 5
10 – 10 = 0
5 + 0 = **5**

Students should understand that multiplication is repeated addition and that division is the grouping of all items into equal sets.

1. Repeated Addition (Multiplication)

Mackenzie eats 2 rolls a day. How many rolls does she eat in 5 days?

$$2 + 2 + 2 + 2 + 2 = 10$$
$$5 \times 2 = 10$$

She eats **10** rolls in 5 days.

2. The Grouping Method (Division)

Mrs. Lee makes 14 sandwiches. She gives all the sandwiches equally to 7 friends. How many sandwiches does each friend receive?

$$14 \div 7 = 2$$

Each friend receives **2** sandwiches.

One of the basic but essential math skills students should acquire is to perform the 4 operations of whole numbers and fractions. Each of these methods is illustrated below.

1. The Adding-Without-Regrouping Method

```
  H  T  O          O: Ones
  3  2  1          T: Tens
+ 5  6  8          H: Hundreds
--------
  8  8  9
```

Since no regrouping is required, add the digits in each place value accordingly.

2. The Adding-by-Regrouping Method

```
  H  T  O          O: Ones
 ¹4  9  2          T: Tens
+ 1  5  3          H: Hundreds
--------
  6  4  5
```

In this example, regroup 14 tens into 1 hundred 4 tens.

3. The Adding-by-Regrouping-Twice Method

$$\begin{array}{ccc} H & T & O \\ {}^12 & {}^18 & 6 \\ + 3 & 6 & 5 \\ \hline 6 & 5 & 1 \end{array}$$

O: Ones
T: Tens
H: Hundreds

Regroup twice in this example.
First, regroup 11 ones into 1 ten 1 one.
Second, regroup 15 tens into 1 hundred 5 tens.

4. The Subtracting-Without-Regrouping Method

$$\begin{array}{ccc} H & T & O \\ 7 & 3 & 9 \\ - 3 & 2 & 5 \\ \hline 4 & 1 & 4 \end{array}$$

O: Ones
T: Tens
H: Hundreds

Since no regrouping is required, subtract the digits in each place value accordingly.

5. The Subtracting-by-Regrouping Method

$$\begin{array}{ccc} H & T & O \\ 5 & {}^7\!8 & {}^{11}\!1 \\ - 2 & 4 & 7 \\ \hline 3 & 3 & 4 \end{array}$$

O: Ones
T: Tens
H: Hundreds

In this example, students cannot subtract 7 ones from 1 one. So, regroup the tens and ones. Regroup 8 tens 1 one into 7 tens 11 ones.

6. The Subtracting-by-Regrouping-Twice Method

$$\begin{array}{ccc} H & T & O \\ {}^7\!8 & {}^9\!0 & {}^{10}\!0 \\ - 5 & 9 & 3 \\ \hline 2 & 0 & 7 \end{array}$$

O: Ones
T: Tens
H: Hundreds

In this example, students cannot subtract 3 ones from 0 ones and 9 tens from 0 tens. So, regroup the hundreds, tens, and ones. Regroup 8 hundreds into 7 hundreds 9 tens 10 ones.

7. The Multiplying-Without-Regrouping Method

$$\begin{array}{cc} T & O \\ 2 & 4 \\ \times & 2 \\ \hline 4 & 8 \end{array}$$

O: Ones
T: Tens

Since no regrouping is required, multiply the digit in each place value by the multiplier accordingly.

8. The Multiplying-With-Regrouping Method

$$\begin{array}{ccc} H & T & O \\ {}^13 & {}^24 & 9 \\ \times & & 3 \\ \hline 1,0 & 4 & 7 \end{array}$$

O: Ones
T: Tens
H: Hundreds

In this example, regroup 27 ones into 2 tens 7 ones, and 14 tens into 1 hundred 4 tens.

9. The Dividing-Without-Regrouping Method

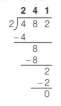

Since no regrouping is required, divide the digit in each place value by the divisor accordingly.

10. The Dividing-With-Regrouping Method

In this example, regroup 3 hundreds into 30 tens and add 3 tens to make 33 tens. Regroup 3 tens into 30 ones.

11. The Addition-of-Fractions Method

$$\frac{1}{6} \times \frac{2}{2} + \frac{1}{4} \times \frac{3}{3} = \frac{2}{12} + \frac{3}{12} = \frac{5}{12}$$

Always remember to make the denominators common before adding the fractions.

12. The Subtraction-of-Fractions Method

$$\frac{1}{2} \times \frac{5}{5} - \frac{1}{5} \times \frac{2}{2} = \frac{5}{10} - \frac{2}{10} = \frac{3}{10}$$

Always remembers to make the denominators common before subtracting the fractions.

13. The Multiplication-of-Fractions Method

$$\frac{{}^1\!3}{5} \times \frac{1}{3_{\,9}} = \frac{1}{15}$$

When the numerator and the denominator have a common multiple, reduce them to their lowest fractions.

14. The Division-of-Fractions Method

$$\frac{7}{9} \div \frac{1}{6} = \frac{7}{3_{\,9}} \times \frac{6^2}{1} = \frac{14}{3} = 4\frac{2}{3}$$

When dividing fractions, first change the division sign (÷) to the multiplication sign (×). Then, switch the numerator and denominator of the fraction on the right hand side. Multiply the fractions in the usual way.

Model drawing is an effective strategy used to solve math word problems. It is a visual representation of the information in word problems using bar units. By drawing the models, students will know of the variables given in the problem, the variables to find, and even the methods used to solve the problem.

Drawing models is also a versatile strategy. It can be applied to simple word problems involving addition, subtraction, multiplication, and division. It can also be applied to word problems related to fractions, decimals, percentage, and ratio.

The use of models also trains students to think in an algebraic manner, which uses symbols for representation.

The different types of bar models used to solve word problems are illustrated below.

1. The model that involves addition

Melissa has 50 blue beads and 20 red beads. How many beads does she have altogether?

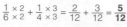

$$50 + 20 = \textbf{70}$$

2. The model that involves subtraction

Ben and Andy have 90 toy cars. Andy has 60 toy cars. How many toy cars does Ben have?

$$90 - 60 = \textbf{30}$$

3. The model that involves comparison

Mr. Simons has 150 magazines and 110 books in his study. How many more magazines than books does he have?

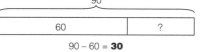

$$150 - 110 = \textbf{40}$$

4. The model that involves two items with a difference

A pair of shoes costs $109. A leather bag costs $241 more than the pair of shoes. How much is the leather bag?

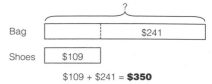

$$\$109 + \$241 = \textbf{\$350}$$

5. The model that involves multiples

Mrs. Drew buys 12 apples. She buys 3 times as many oranges as apples. She also buys 3 times as many cherries as oranges. How many pieces of fruit does she buy altogether?

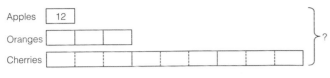

$$13 \times 12 = \mathbf{156}$$

6. The model that involves multiples and difference

There are 15 students in Class A. There are 5 more students in Class B than in Class A. There are 3 times as many students in Class C than in Class A. How many students are there altogether in the three classes?

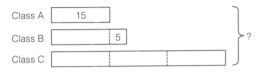

$$(5 \times 15) + 5 = \mathbf{80}$$

7. The model that involves creating a whole

Ellen, Giselle, and Brenda bake 111 muffins. Giselle bakes twice as many muffins as Brenda. Ellen bakes 9 fewer muffins than Giselle. How many muffins does Ellen bake?

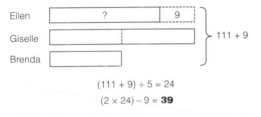

$$(111 + 9) \div 5 = 24$$
$$(2 \times 24) - 9 = \mathbf{39}$$

8. The model that involves sharing

There are 183 tennis balls in Basket A and 97 tennis balls in Basket B. How many tennis balls must be transferred from Basket A to Basket B so that both baskets contain the same number of tennis balls?

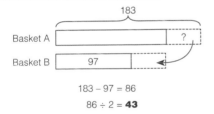

$$183 - 97 = 86$$
$$86 \div 2 = \mathbf{43}$$

9. The model that involves fractions

George had 355 marbles. He lost $\frac{1}{5}$ of the marbles and gave $\frac{1}{4}$ of the remaining marbles to his brother. How many marbles did he have left?

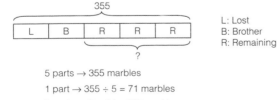

L: Lost
B: Brother
R: Remaining

5 parts → 355 marbles
1 part → 355 ÷ 5 = 71 marbles
3 parts → 3 × 71 = **213** marbles

10. The model that involves ratio

Aaron buys a tie and a belt. The prices of the tie and belt are in the ratio 2 : 5. If both items cost $539,

(a) what is the price of the tie?

(b) what is the price of the belt?

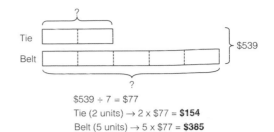

$$\$539 \div 7 = \$77$$
Tie (2 units) → 2 × $77 = **$154**
Belt (5 units) → 5 × $77 = **$385**

11. The model that involves comparison of fractions

Jack's height is $\frac{2}{3}$ of Leslie's height. Leslie's height is $\frac{3}{4}$ of Lindsay's height. If Lindsay is 160 cm tall, find Jack's height and Leslie's height.

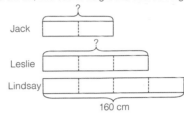

1 unit → 160 ÷ 4 = 40 cm

Leslie's height (3 units) → 3 × 40 = **120 cm**

Jack's height (2 units) → 2 × 40 = **80 cm**

Thinking skills and strategies are important in mathematical problem solving. These skills are applied when students think through the math problems to solve them. Below are some commonly used thinking skills and strategies applied in mathematical problem solving.

1. Comparing

Comparing is a form of thinking skill that students can apply to identify similarities and differences.

When comparing numbers, look carefully at each digit before deciding if a number is greater or less than the other. Students might also use a number line for comparison when there are more numbers.

Example:

3 is greater than 2 but smaller than 7.

2. Sequencing

A sequence shows the order of a series of numbers. *Sequencing* is a form of thinking skill that requires students to place numbers in a particular order. There are many terms in a sequence. The terms refer to the numbers in a sequence.

To place numbers in a correct order, students must first find a rule that generates the sequence. In a simple math sequence, students can either add or subtract to find the unknown terms in the sequence.

Example: Find the 7th term in the sequence below.

1,	4,	7,	10,	13,	16	?
1st term	2nd term	3rd term	4th term	5th term	6th term	7th term

Step 1: This sequence is in an increasing order.
Step 2: 4 − 1 = 3   7 − 4 = 3
The difference between two consecutive terms is 3.
Step 3: 16 + 3 = 19
The 7th term is **19**.

3. Visualization

Visualization is a problem solving strategy that can help students visualize a problem through the use of physical objects. Students will play a more active role in solving the problem by manipulating these objects.

The main advantage of using this strategy is the mobility of information in the process of solving the problem. When students make a wrong step in the process, they can retrace the step without erasing or canceling it.

The other advantage is that this strategy helps develop a better understanding of the problem or solution through visual objects or images. In this way, students will be better able to remember how to solve these types of problems.

...of the commonly used objects for this strategy are toothpicks, straws, strings, water, sand, pencils, paper, and dice.

Look for a Pattern

This strategy requires the use of observational and analytical skills. Students have to observe the given data to find a pattern in order to solve the problem. Math word problems that involve the use of this strategy usually have repeated numbers or patterns.

Example: Find the sum of all the numbers from 1 to 100.

Step 1: <u>Simplify the problem.</u>
Find the sum of 1, 2, 3, 4, 5, 6, 7, 8, 9, and 10.

Step 2: <u>Look for a pattern.</u>

1 + 10 = 11	2 + 9 = 11	3 + 8 = 11
4 + 7 = 11	5 + 6 = 11	

Step 3: <u>Describe the pattern.</u>
When finding the sum of 1 to 10, add the first and last numbers to get a result of 11. Then, add the second and second last numbers to get the same result. The pattern continues until all the numbers from 1 to 10 are added. There will be 5 pairs of such results. Since each addition equals 11, the answer is then 5 × 11 = 55.

Step 4: <u>Use the pattern to find the answer.</u>
Since there are 5 pairs in the sum of 1 to 10, there should be (10 × 5 = 50 pairs) in the sum of 1 to 100.
Note that the addition for each pair is not equal to 11 now. The addition for each pair is now (1 + 100 = 101).
50 × 101 = 5050
The sum of all the numbers from 1 to 100 is **5,050**.

5. Working Backward

The strategy of working backward applies only to a specific type of math word problem. These word problems state the end result, and students are required to find the total number. In order to solve these word problems, students have to work backward by thinking through the correct sequence of events. The strategy of working backward allows students to use their logical reasoning and sequencing to find the answers.

Example: Sarah has a piece of ribbon. She cuts the ribbon into 4 equal parts. Each part is then cut into 3 smaller equal parts. If the length of each small part is 35 cm, how long is the piece of ribbon?
3 × 35 = 105 cm
4 × 105 = 420 cm
The piece of ribbon is **420 cm**.

6. The Before-After Concept

The *Before-After* concept lists all the relevant data before and after an event. Students can then compare the differences and eventually solve the problems. Usually, the Before-After concept and the mathematical model go hand in hand to solve math word problems. Note that the Before-After concept can be applied only to a certain type of math word problem, which trains students to think sequentially.

Example: Kelly has 4 times as much money as Joey. After Kelly uses some money to buy a tennis racquet, and Joey uses $30 to buy a pair of pants, Kelly has twice as much money as Joey. If Joey has $98 in the beginning,
(a) how much money does Kelly have in the end?
(b) how much money does Kelly spend on the tennis racquet?

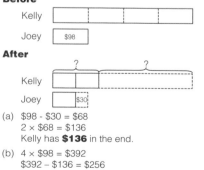

(a) $98 - $30 = $68
2 × $68 = $136
Kelly has **$136** in the end.
(b) 4 × $98 = $392
$392 – $136 = $256
Kelly spends **$256** on the tennis racquet.

7. Making Supposition

Making supposition is commonly known as "making an assumption." Students can use this strategy to solve certain types of math word problems. Making

assumptions will eliminate some possibilities and simplifies the word problems by providing a boundary of values to work within.

Example: Mrs. Jackson bought 100 pieces of candy for all the students in her class. How many pieces of candy would each student receive if there were 25 students in her class?

In the above word problem, assume that each student received the same number of pieces. This eliminates the possibilities that some students would receive more than others due to good behaviour, better results, or any other reason.

8. Representation of Problem

In problem solving, students often use representations in the solutions to show their understanding of the problems. Using representations also allow students to understand the mathematical concepts and relationships as well as to manipulate the information presented in the problems. Examples of representations are diagrams and lists or tables.

Diagrams allow students to consolidate or organize the information given in the problems. By drawing a diagram, students can see the problem clearly and solve it effectively.

A list or table can help students organize information that is useful for analysis. After analyzing, students can then see a pattern, which can be used to solve the problem.

9. Guess and Check

One of the most important and effective problem-solving techniques is *Guess and Check*. It is also known as *Trial and Error*. As the name suggests, students have to guess the answer to a problem and check if that guess is correct. If the guess is wrong, students will make another guess. This will continue until the guess is correct.

It is beneficial to keep a record of all the guesses and checks in a table. In addition, a *Comments* column can be included. This will enable students to analyze their guess (if it is too high or too low) and improve on the next guess. Be careful; this problem-solving technique can be tiresome without systematic or logical guesses.

Example: Jessica had 15 coins. Some of them were 10-cent coins and the rest were 5-cent coins. The total amount added up to $1.25. How many coins of each kind were there?

Use the guess-and-check method.

Number of 10¢ Coins	Value	Number of 5¢ Coins	Value	Total Number of Coins	Total Value
7	7 × 10¢ = 70¢	8	8 × 5¢ = 40¢	7 + 8 = 15	70¢ + 40¢ = 110¢ = $1.10
8	8 × 10¢ = 80¢	7	7 × 5¢ = 35¢	8 + 7 = 15	80¢ + 35¢ = 115¢ = $1.15
10	10 × 10¢ = 100¢	5	5 × 5¢ = 25¢	10 + 5 = 15	100¢ + 25¢ = 125¢ = $1.25

There were **ten** 10-cent coins and **five** 5-cent coins.

10. Restate the Problem

When solving challenging math problems, conventional methods may not be workable. Instead, restating the problem will enable students to see some challenging problems in a different light so that they can better understand them.

The strategy of restating the problem is to "say" the problem in a different and clearer way. However, students have to ensure that the main idea of the problem is not altered.

How do students restate a math problem?

First, read and understand the problem. Gather the given facts and unknowns. Note any condition(s) that have to be satisfied.

Next, restate the problem. Imagine narrating this problem to a friend. Present the given facts, unknown(s), and condition(s). Students may want to write the "revised" problem. Once the "revised" problem is analyzed, students should be able to think of an appropriate strategy to solve it.

11. Simplify the Problem

One of the commonly used strategies in mathematical problem solving is simplification of the problem. When a problem is simplified, it can be "broken down" into two or more smaller parts. Students can then solve the parts systematically to get to the final answer.

Table of Contents

2 diamond rings and 4 silver rings cost $1,440. A diamond ring and a silver ring cost $660. How much does a silver ring cost?

$d + s = 660$
$s = 660 - d$

$1,440$
$- \ \ 660$
$\overline{\ \ \ 780}$

Total cost is 1,440

$d + s + s + s + s = 1440$

$d + d + s + s + s + s = 1440$
660

$2d$

$d + 660 + 3s = 1440$

$d + 3s = 1440 - 660$

$d + 3s = 780$

$d + 3(660 - d) = 780$

$d +$

$d + d$

$s + s + s + s$

$660 \times 3 = 980$

Answer: _____60_____

Name_____

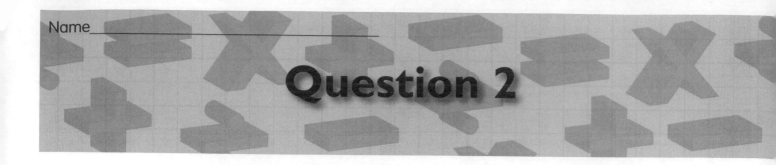

Logan and Izzy had the same number of stickers. After Izzy gave him 72 stickers, Logan had 3 times as many stickers as Izzy. How many stickers did they have altogether?

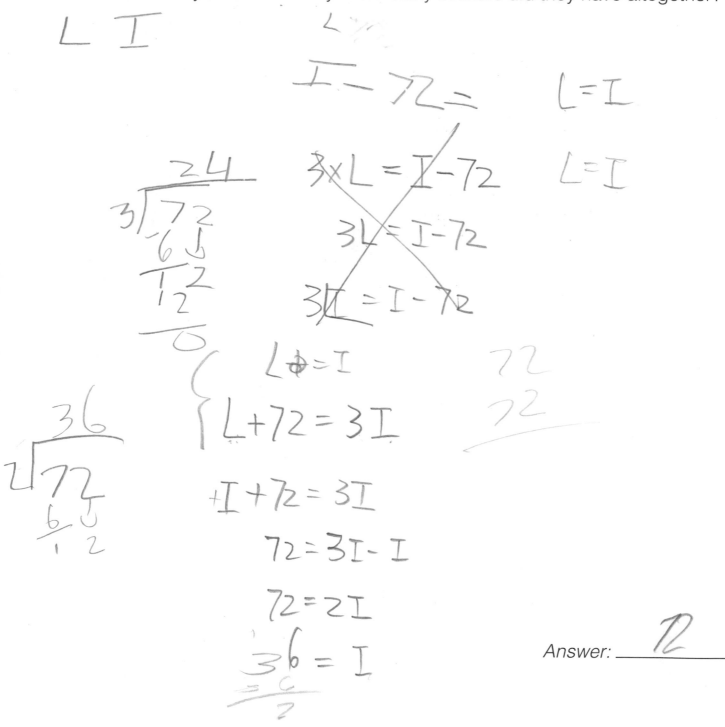

$L \quad I$

$I - 72 =$

$L = I$

$3 \times L = I - 72 \qquad L = I$

$3L = I - 72$

$3L = I - 72$

$L = I$

$\begin{cases} L + 72 = 3I \end{cases}$

72
72

$I + 72 = 3I$

$72 = 3I - I$

$72 = 2I$

$36 = I$

$\begin{array}{r} 24 \\ 3\overline{)72} \\ -6 \\ \overline{12} \\ 12 \\ \overline{0} \end{array}$

$\begin{array}{r} 36 \\ 2\overline{)72} \\ 6 \\ 12 \end{array}$

Answer: _____72_____

David and Amrita had an equal number of marbles. After Amrita gave 50 marbles to David, he had 5 times as many marbles as her Find the total number of marbles they had.

D=A

5×50

A – 5c =

5D = A – 50

FD = A – 50

50 = A – 50

50 – D = 5

50 – D = 40

Answer: 160

Soo-Jin and Mary had an equal number of beads. After Soo-Jin gave 54 beads to Mary, Mary had 7 times as many beads as Soo-Jin. How many beads did they have altogether?

Answer: _____

Antonio and Abby had the same number of paperclips. After Antonio gave 30 paperclips to Abby, Abby had twice as many paperclips as Antonio. How many paperclips did they have in all?

Answer: _____

Emily and Jasmine had the same number of stamps. After Emily gave 42 stamps to Jasmine, Jasmine had twice as many stamps as Emily. How many stamps did Jasmine have in the end?

Answer: _____

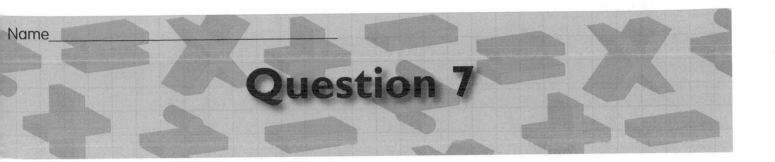

Question 7

Elena has 60 colored pencils. Lucy has 26 colored pencils. How many pencils must Elena give to Lucy so that Elena will have 4 more colored pencils than Lucy?

Answer: _____

Question 8

Dylan, Michael, and Jeremy had $171. Michael had twice as much money as Dylan. Jeremy had 3 times as much money as Michael. How much money did Jeremy have?

Answer: _____

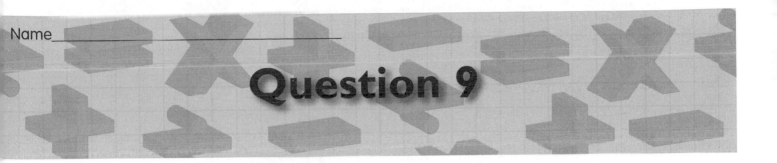

Question 9

Andy and Ben had a total of $60. If Andy gave Ben $8, they would have an equal amount of money. How much money did Ben have in the beginning?

Answer: _____

Question 10

Maddy had twice as many stamps as Simon. After Maddy sold 60 stamps, Simon had twice as many stamps as Maddy. How many more stamps did Maddy have than Simon in the beginning?

Answer: _____

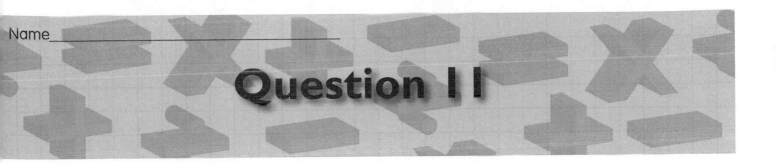

Question 11

Mrs. Owen ordered 500 chicken wings to be shared equally among 250 guests invited to her wedding anniversary party. However, the turnout was less than expected, and every guest ate one more chicken wing than originally planned. If there were 92 chicken wings left after the party, how many people attended Mrs. Owen's party?

Answer: _____

Question 12

The total number of cherries on a plate, in a cup, and in a bowl is 780. The plate contains 145 cherries. The number of cherries in the bowl is 4 times the total number of cherries on the plate and in the cup. How many cherries are in the cup?

Answer: _____

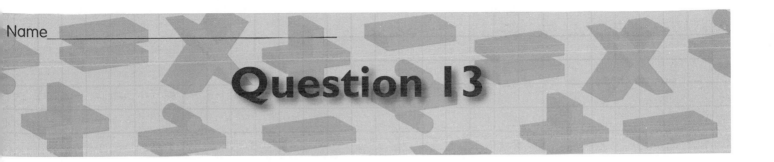

Question 13

Omar is 3 times as old as Jason. Henry is 5 years older than Jason. If their total age is 80 years old, how much older is Omar than Henry?

Answer: _____

Question 14

Mrs. Anderson had twice as many chickens as ducks. She sold 272 chickens and 16 ducks. She then had half as many chickens as ducks. How many chickens did she have in the beginning?

Answer: _____

Question 15

Mrs. Ortega paid $188 for some jeans and T-shirts. A pair of jeans cost $26, and a T- shirt was $16 cheaper than a pair of jeans. If Mrs. Ortega bought 3 pairs of jeans, how many T-shirts did she buy?

Answer: _____

Carmen had $130 more than her sister, Rosa. Rosa had twice as much money as their youngest sister, Zoe. If their mother gave Carmen $60 and Rosa $80, Carmen would have twice as much money as Rosa. What was the total amount of money they had in the beginning?

Answer: _____

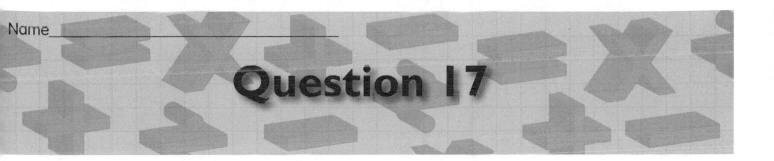

Question 17

Kenji, James, and Ethan shared 240 stickers. Kenji received twice as many stickers as James. James received 3 times as many stickers as Ethan. How many stickers did Kenji receive?

Answer: _____

Question 18

Mrs. Rothberg baked 500 muffins on Saturday and 3 times as many muffins on Sunday. If she sold 5 muffins for $4, how much would she earn by selling all her muffins on both days?

Answer: _____

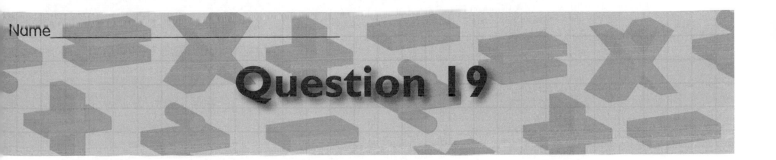

Question 19

Jack had $80 more than Eric. When Jack spent $30, he found that the amount of money he had left was twice as much as what Eric had. How much did the boys have altogether in the beginning?

Answer: _____

Question 20

A shirt cost $15 more than a pair of shorts. Terrell paid $101 for 3 shirts and 5 pairs of shorts. How much did each shirt cost?

Answer: _____

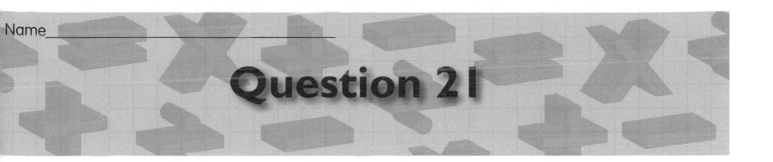

A watch costs $48 more than a clock. The cost of the clock is $\frac{4}{7}$ the cost of the watch. Find the total cost of the 2 items.

Answer: _____

Sam had 70 erasers and rulers. After giving away $\frac{1}{3}$ of his erasers and 10 rulers, he had an equal number of erasers and rulers left. How many erasers did he have in the beginning?

Answer: _____

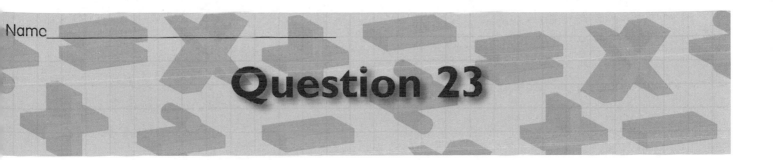
A farmer had a total of 700 goats and sheep. If he sold $\frac{3}{4}$ of his goats and 400 sheep, he would have an equal number of goats and sheep left. How many more sheep than goats did he have in the beginning?

Answer: _____

Question 24

In a factory, the number of female workers is $3\frac{2}{3}$ times the number of male workers. There are 16 more female than male workers. Find the total number of workers in the factory.

Answer: _____

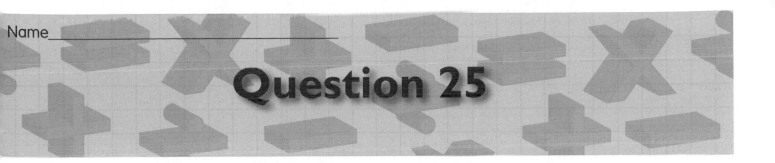

Nikhil had $\frac{3}{7}$ as many books as William. They had a total of 340 books. How many books must William give to Nikhil so that each of them would have the same number of books?

Answer: _____

Question 26

Mrs. Yang bought 5 chickens and 3 ducks for $81. A chicken cost $5 more than a duck.

(a)   What was the cost of each duck?

(b)   What was the cost of each chicken?

Answer: (a) _____

(b) _____

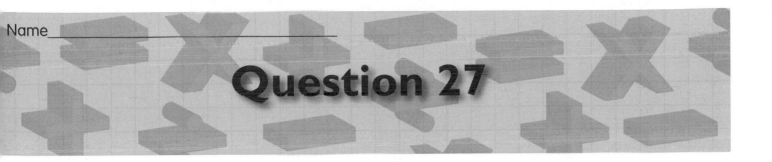

Kelly bought 4 apples and 6 pears for $5. Jocy bought 8 apples and 2 pears for $4. Find the price of an apple.

Answer: _____

Question 28

Find a number that is more than 50 but less than 100. When the number is divided by 7, the remainder is 4. When the number is divided by 10, the remainder is 8. What is the number?

Answer: _____

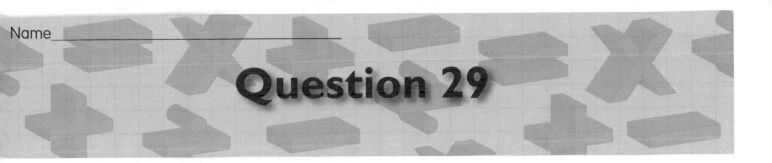

Meera paid $240 for 4 pairs of shoes and 4 pairs of shorts. Each pair of shoes cost 4 times as much as a pair of shorts. Find the difference in price between a pair of shoes and a pair of shorts.

Answer: _____

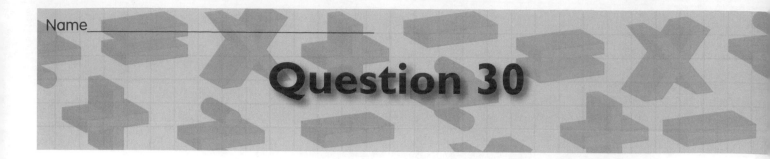

Question 30

Aunt Jane is 31 years old. Her daughter is 13 years old. How many years ago was Aunt Jane 3 times as old as her daughter?

Answer: _____

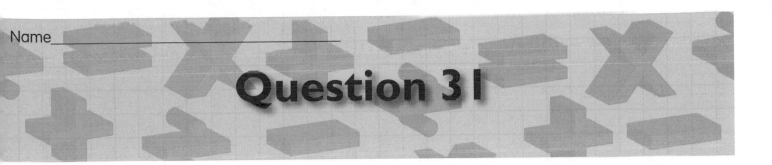

Question 31

Caleb had 90 pencils and pens. After giving away $\frac{1}{3}$ of his pencils and 10 pens, he had an equal number of pencils and pens left. How many pencils did he have in the beginning?

Answer: _____

Question 32

The sum of Mr. O'Malley's age and his son's age is 38 years this year. 4 years ago, Mr. O'Malley was 5 times as old as his son.

(a)   How old is his son this year?

(b)   How old is Mr. O'Malley this year?

Answer: (a) _____

(b) _____

Name_____

Question 33

This year, Albert and his grandfather's ages total 64 years. In 3 years, Albert's grandfather will be 6 times as old as Albert. How many years older than Albert is his grandfather this year?

Answer: _____

Name_____

Question 34

I am a number between 60 and 80. I have a remainder of 3 when divided by 4. I have a remainder of 1 when divided by 7. What number am I?

Answer: _____

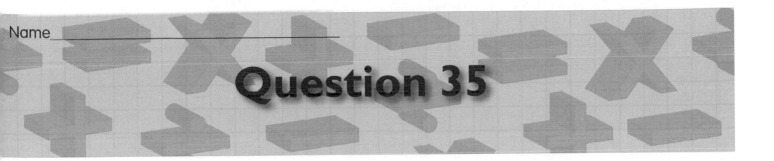

Question 35

When a number is divided by 3, the remainder is 1. When the same number is divided by 4, the remainder is 2. If the number is between 50 and 60, what is the number?

Answer: _____

Question 36

Sarah spent $\frac{4}{9}$ of her paycheck on food, $\frac{1}{3}$ of her remaining money on rent, $180 on shopping, $270 on clothing, and saved the remaining $50. What fraction of her paycheck did she save?

Answer: _____

Name_____

Question 37

Carter and Ari had $240 altogether. Ari had twice as much as Carter after Carter gave him $16. How much more money did Ari have than Carter in the beginning?

Answer: _____

Question 38

8 shirts and 5 pairs of pants cost $695 altogether. 3 shirts and 3 pairs of pants cost $300 altogether. How much more does each shirt cost than each pair of pants?

Answer: _____

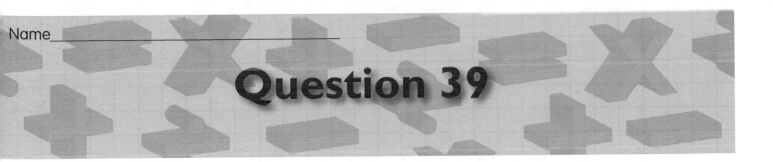

Ella and Nico had $250 altogether. If Nico spent $35, he would still have $5 more than Ella. How much money did Ella have?

Answer: _____

Question 40

Manuel had some marbles. He gave Lily half of his marbles plus 1 more. He gave Matt half of the remaining marbles plus 2 more. If he had 5 marbles left in the end, how many marbles did Manuel have in the beginning?

Answer: _____

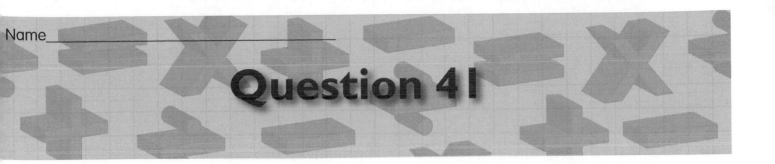

Question 41

Xavier, Thomas, and Mei had 650 marbles. Thomas had 3 times as many marbles as Mei. Mei had 50 fewer marbles than Xavier. How many marbles did Xavier and Mei have altogether?

Answer: _____

Question 42

There were an equal number of boys and girls in a school auditorium. After 24 boys left the auditorium, there were 3 times as many girls as boys. How many children were there in the beginning?

Answer: _____

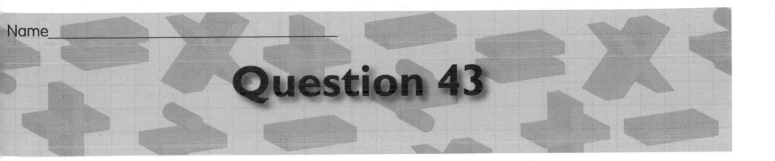

Nathan and Audrey had $250. After Audrey gave $10 to Nathan, they had the same amount of money left. How much money did Nathan have in the beginning?

Answer: _____

Question 44

8 waffles cost $4 more than 8 pancakes. Harry paid $18 for 4 pancakes and 4 waffles. What was the cost of a pancake?

Answer: _____

The cost of an angelfish and a goldfish was $8. Adam bought 6 angelfish, 2 goldfish, and a swordtail for $34. If the total cost of an angelfish and a swordtail was $10.50, what was the cost of a goldfish?

Answer: _____

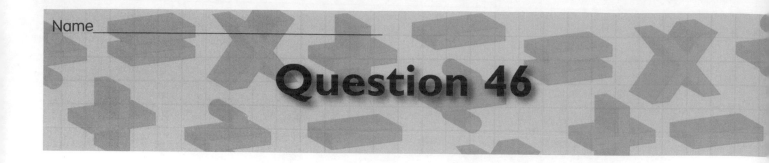

Question 46

Luisa and Sierra had 19 stamps. After Sierra gave Luisa 2 stamps, Sierra had 1 more stamp than Luisa. How many stamps did Sierra have in the beginning?

Answer: _____

Name_____

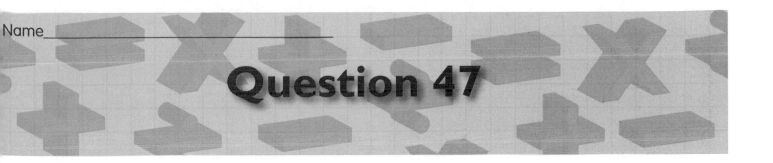

Austin spent an equal amount of money on 5 DVDs and 7 CDs. Each DVD cost 30 cents more than each CD. How much did Austin spend altogether?

Answer: _____

Question 48

Rashad had ducks and cows on his farm. These 14 animals had a total of 40 legs. How many cows and ducks were there?

Answer: _____

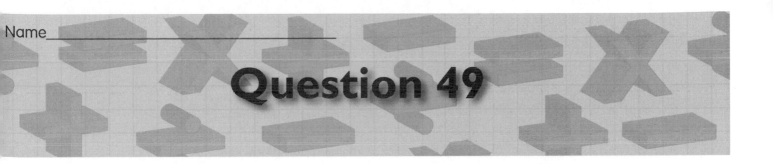

Question 49

Benjamin has 10 bills that add up to $320. Some are 50-dollar bills, and the rest are 20-dollar bills. How many 50-dollar bills and 20-dollar bills does he have?

Answer: _____

Question 50

Mr. Sanders had 20 bills. Some of them were 5-dollar bills, and the rest were 20-dollar bills. The total value of the bills was $220. How many bills of each kind were there?

Answer: _____

Jeremy bought 16 boxes of crayons, with each box containing 15 crayons. He gave all the crayons to 20 children during a birthday party. There were 4 more boys than girls. If each child received the same number of crayons, how many more crayons did the boys receive than the girls?

Answer: _____

Question 52

Takashi spent $\frac{1}{3}$ of his money on a jacket. He spent $\frac{1}{4}$ of the remaining money on a pair of boots. If the pair of boots cost $35 less than the jacket, how much money did he have in the beginning?

Answer: _____

Question 53

2 boxes of salt and a box of sugar cost $6.60. A box of salt is $1.20 less than a box of sugar. What is the cost of a box of sugar?

Answer: _____

Question 54

June bought 5 mechanical pencils and some pens at a stationery shop. Each mechanical pencil cost $4. Each pen cost $10 less than 5 mechanical pencils. If June spent $90, how many pens did she buy?

Answer: _____

Question 55

Max and his two brothers, Sean and Kennedy, received a sum of money. Max received 3 times as much as Sean. Max received $400 more than Kennedy. If Sean received $280, what was the total amount of money the 3 brothers received?

Answer: _____

Kyra has 175 pieces of colored paper. Rico has 3 times as many pieces as Kyra. Grace has twice as many pieces as Rico. How many pieces of colored paper does Grace have?

Answer: _____

Name_____

Blake bought 5 books and 9 file folders. He gave the cashier $50 and received $2.05 in change. If each book cost $6.35, what was the cost of each file folder?

Answer: _____

Question 58

Stephen has 356 pennies. Jess has 136 more pennies than Stephen. Tommy has twice as many pennies as Jess. How many pennies do they have altogether?

Answer: _____

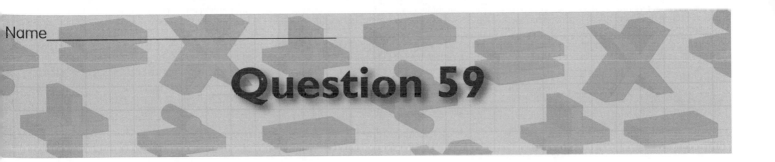

Question 59

Mr. Knapp had some stamps. If he gave 7 stamps to each of his children, he would have 5 stamps left. If he gave 8 stamps to each child, he would need 3 more stamps in order for the children to have an equal number of stamps. How many stamps did Mr. Knapp have?

Answer: _____

Question 60

Mrs. Reyes had some apples. If she gave each student 3 apples, she would have 2 apples left. If she gave each student 4 apples, she would be short 2 apples. How many apples did she have?

Answer: _____

$\frac{3}{10}$ of the people in a supermarket are children. There are 84 adults.

(a)   How many people are in the supermarket altogether?

(b)   How many more adults than children are there?

Answer: (a) _____

(b) _____

$\frac{3}{11}$ of the people in the audience at a concert hall are children. There are 800 more adults than children.

(a)   How many people are at the concert hall?

(b) $\frac{3}{8}$ of the children are girls. How many more boys than girls are there?

Answer: (a) _____

(b) _____

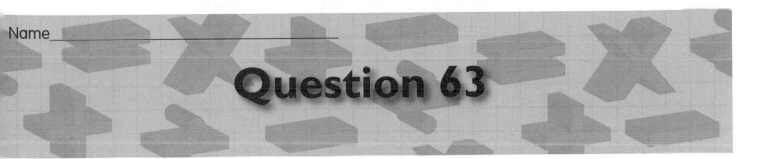

There were a total of 800 novels and nonfiction books at a bookshop. $\frac{2}{5}$ of these books were novels. Each novel was priced at $7. Each nonfiction book was priced at $5. How much money would the owner of the bookshop make if he sold $\frac{3}{8}$ of the novels and $\frac{2}{5}$ of the nonfiction books?

Answer: _____

Question 64

There was a total of 400 oranges and mangoes at a fruit stall. $\frac{3}{8}$ of these fruits were mangoes. Each orange was priced at 40 cents, and each mango was priced at 60 cents. How much would Mr. Mead make if he sold $\frac{2}{3}$ of the mangoes and $\frac{4}{5}$ of the oranges?

Answer: _____

Allison has $3\frac{1}{3}$ times as many stickers as Sophia. Sophia has 18 stickers. How many stickers do they have altogether?

Answer: _____

Question 66

A pineapple and 4 oranges cost $8.40. The pineapple costs $5.90 more than an orange. Find the cost of the pineapple.

Answer: _____

Question 67

Brady gave $\frac{1}{5}$ of his paycheck to his mother and spent $\frac{1}{2}$ of the remainder on a radio. He had $450 left. How much was his paycheck?

Answer: _____

A rope is 20.85 m long. Two pieces of 1.85 m each are cut from it, and the remainder is cut into 7 equal pieces. How long is each of the 7 equal pieces of rope?

Answer: _____

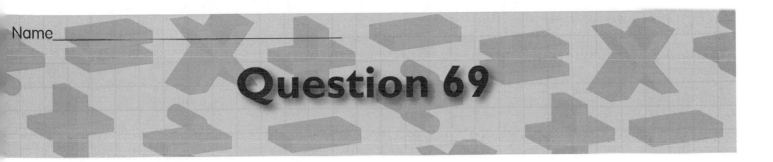

Question 69

A painting measures 30 in. by 20 in. The border around the painting is 3 in. wide. Find the area of the border.

Answer: _____

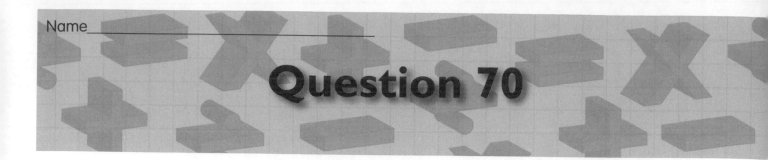
At a movie, $\frac{1}{4}$ of the people in the theater were men, $\frac{5}{8}$ were women, and the rest were children. If there were 100 more women than children, what was the total number of people in the theater?

Answer: _____

Solutions to
Word Problems
1-70

Since 1 diamond ring and 1 silver ring cost $660,

> Use the multiplying-with-regrouping method.

$660 × 2 = $1,320

```
      1
    6 6 0
  ×     2
  1, 3 2 0
```

2 diamond rings and 2 silver rings cost $1,320.

> Use the subtracting-without-regrouping method.

$1,440 − $1,320 = $120

```
  1, 4 4 0
− 1, 3 2 0
    1 2 0
```

2 silver rings cost $120.

> Use the dividing-with-regrouping method.

$120 ÷ 2 = $60

```
        6 0
  2 ⟌ 1 2 0
    − 1 2
          0
        − 0
          0
```

A silver ring costs **$60**.

Answer: ___**$60**___

Solution to Question 2

Since Logan had 3 times as many stickers after, Logan and Izzy shared 4 parts equally at first.

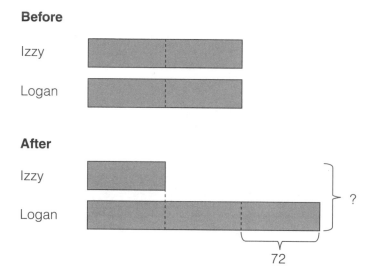

Before

Izzy

Logan

After

Izzy

Logan

?

72

Each part is 72 stickers.

Total number of stickers = 4 parts

Use the multiplying-without-regrouping method.

$72 \times 4 = 288$

$$\begin{array}{r} 7\ 2 \\ \times\quad 4 \\ \hline 2\ 8\ 8 \end{array}$$

They had **288** stickers altogether.

Answer: __**288 stickers**__

Since David had 5 times as many marbles after, David and Amrita shared 6 parts equally at first.

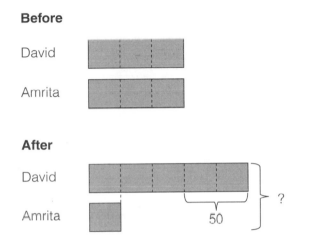

Before

David

Amrita

After

David

Amrita

50

?

Since 2 equal parts are 50,

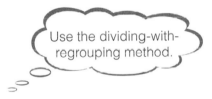

Use the dividing-with-regrouping method.

$$50 \div 2 = 25$$

$$\begin{array}{r} 25 \\ 2\overline{)50} \\ -4 \\ \hline 10 \\ -10 \\ \hline 0 \end{array}$$

each part is 25.

Use the multiplying-with-regrouping method.

6 parts = 25 × 6 = 150

$$\begin{array}{r} \overset{3}{2}\,5 \\ \times \quad 6 \\ \hline 1\,5\,0 \end{array}$$

They had a total of marbles.

Answer: __**150 marbles**__

Since Mary had 7 times as many beads after, Mary and Soo-Jin shared 8 parts equally at first.

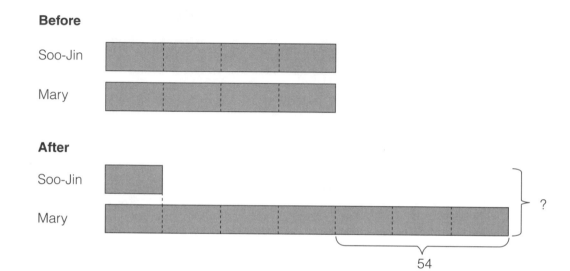

Before

Soo-Jin

Mary

After

Soo-Jin

Mary

?

54

Since 3 equal parts are 54,

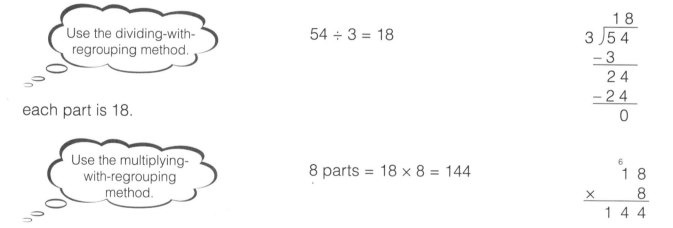

Use the dividing-with-regrouping method.

$54 \div 3 = 18$

$$\begin{array}{r} 18 \\ 3\overline{)54} \\ -3 \\ \hline 24 \\ -24 \\ \hline 0 \end{array}$$

each part is 18.

Use the multiplying-with-regrouping method.

8 parts = $18 \times 8 = 144$

$$\begin{array}{r} {}^{6}18 \\ \times 8 \\ \hline 144 \end{array}$$

They had **144** beads altogether.

Answer: ___**144 beads**___

Before

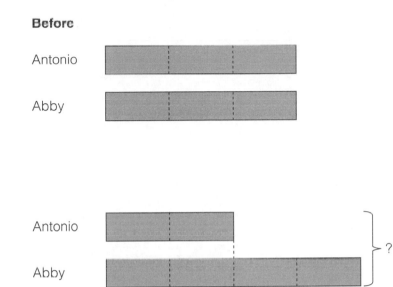

Antonio

Abby

Each part is 30.

Use the multiplying-without-regrouping method.

6 parts – 30 × 6 = 180

$$\begin{array}{r} 3\ 0 \\ \times\ \ \ \ 6 \\ \hline 1\ 8\ 0 \end{array}$$

They had **180** paperclips in all.

Answer: **180 paperclips**

Before

Emily

Jasmine

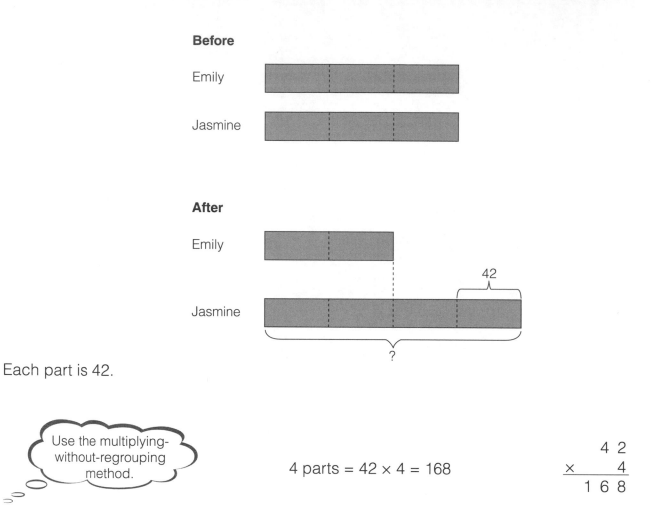

After

Emily

42

Jasmine

?

Each part is 42.

Use the multiplying-without-regrouping method.

4 parts = 42 × 4 = 168

```
    4 2
×     4
  1 6 8
```

Jasmine had **168** stamps in the end.

Answer: **168 stamps**

Use the adding-without-regrouping method.

$$60 + 26 = 86$$

They have 86 colored pencils altogether.

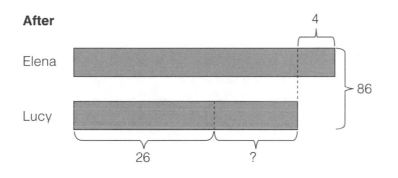

After

Elena

Lucy

4

86

26

?

$$86 - 4 = 82$$

Since 2 equal parts are 82,

Use the dividing-with-regrouping method.

$$82 \div 2 = 41$$

$$
\begin{array}{r}
4\ 1 \\
2\overline{)8\ 2} \\
-8 \\
\hline
2 \\
-2 \\
\hline
0
\end{array}
$$

each part is 41.

Lucy will have 41 colored pencils if Elena has 4 more pencils than her.

Use the subtracting-by-regrouping method.

$$41 - 26 = 15$$

$$
\begin{array}{r}
^{3}\cancel{4}\ ^{11}\cancel{1} \\
-\ 2\ 6 \\
\hline
1\ 5
\end{array}
$$

Elena must give Lucy **15** colored pencils.

Answer: **15 colored pencils**

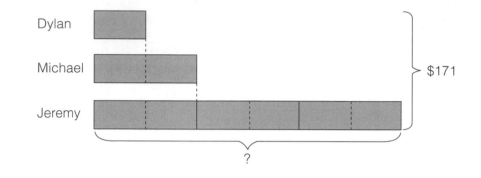

9 parts = $171

Use the dividing-with-regrouping method.

1 part = $171 ÷ 9 = $19

```
        1 9
   9 ) 1 7 1
     -  9
        8 1
      - 8 1
          0
```

Use the multiplying-with-regrouping method.

6 parts = $19 × 6 = $114

```
       5
       1 9
   ×     6
   1 1 4
```

Jeremy had **$114**.

Answer: **$114**

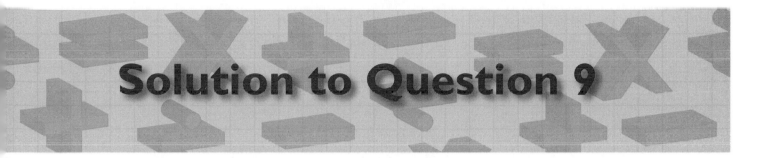

Use the dividing-with-regrouping method.

$60 ÷ 2 = $30

$$\begin{array}{r} 30 \\ 2\overline{)60} \\ -6 \\ \hline 0 \\ -0 \\ \hline 0 \end{array}$$

Ben had $30 in the end.

Use the subtracting-by-regrouping method.

$30 – $8 – $22

Ben had **$22** in the beginning.

Answer: _____**$22**_____

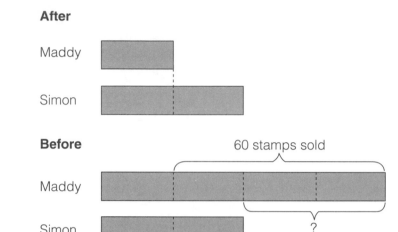

After

Maddy

Simon

Before

60 stamps sold

Maddy

Simon

?

Since 3 equal parts are 60,

Use the dividing-with-regrouping method.

$60 \div 3 = 20$

$$\begin{array}{r} 20 \\ 3\overline{)60} \\ -6 \\ \hline 0 \\ -0 \\ \hline 0 \end{array}$$

each part is 20.

Use the multiplying-without-regrouping method.

2 parts = $20 \times 2 = 40$

$$\begin{array}{r} 20 \\ \times2 \\ \hline 40 \end{array}$$

Maddy had **40** more stamps than Simon in the beginning.

Answer: **40 more stamps**

$2 \times 25 = 50$

$500 \div 250 = 50 \div 25 = 2$

Mrs. Owen planned that each guest would eat 2 chicken wings.

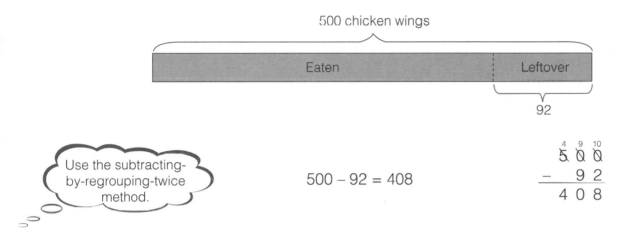

500 chicken wings

| Eaten | Leftover |

92

Use the subtracting-by-regrouping-twice method.

$500 - 92 = 408$

$$\begin{array}{r} \overset{4}{\cancel{5}}\,\overset{9}{\cancel{0}}\,\overset{10}{\cancel{0}} \\ -\quad 9\;2 \\ \hline 4\;0\;8 \end{array}$$

The guests ate 408 chicken wings.

Each guest ate 3 chicken wings at the party.

Use the dividing-with-regrouping method.

$408 \div 3 = 136$

$$\begin{array}{r} 136 \\ 3\overline{)408} \\ -3 \\ \hline 10 \\ -9 \\ \hline 18 \\ -18 \\ \hline 0 \end{array}$$

136 people attended Mrs. Owen's party.

Answer: __**136 people**__

Since 5 equal parts are 780,

$$780 \div 5 = 156$$

$$
\begin{array}{r}
156 \\
5\overline{)780} \\
-5 \\
\hline
28 \\
-25 \\
\hline
30 \\
-30 \\
\hline
0
\end{array}
$$

each part is 156.

There are 156 cherries on the plate and in the cup.

Use the subtracting-without-regrouping method.

$$156 - 145 = 11$$

$$
\begin{array}{r}
156 \\
-145 \\
\hline
11
\end{array}
$$

There are **11** cherries in the cup.

Answer: **11 cherries**

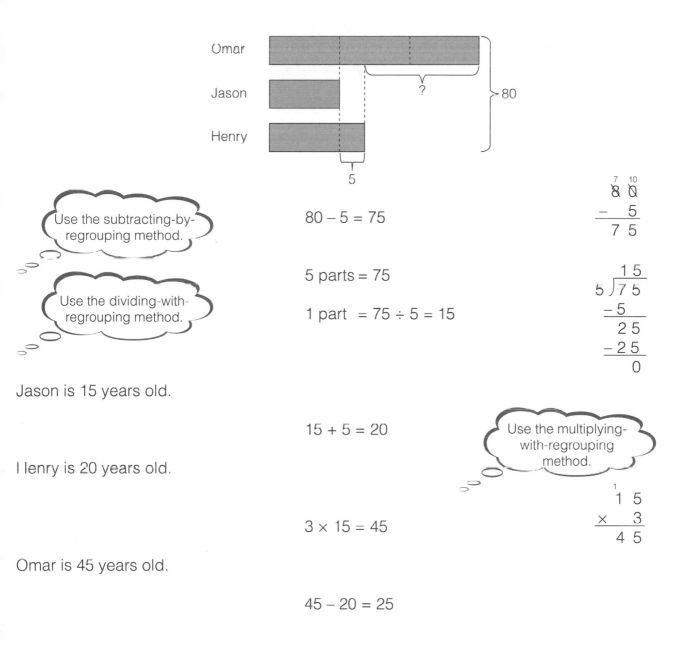

Use the subtracting-by-regrouping method.

Use the dividing-with-regrouping method.

$80 - 5 = 75$

$$\begin{array}{r} {\scriptstyle 7\ \ 10} \\ \cancel{8}\ \cancel{0} \\ -\quad 5 \\ \hline 7\ 5 \end{array}$$

5 parts = 75

1 part $= 75 \div 5 = 15$

$$\begin{array}{r} 1\ 5 \\ 5\,\overline{)7\ 5} \\ -5 \\ \hline 2\ 5 \\ -2\ 5 \\ \hline 0 \end{array}$$

Jason is 15 years old.

$15 + 5 = 20$

Use the multiplying-with-regrouping method.

Henry is 20 years old.

$3 \times 15 = 45$

$$\begin{array}{r} {\scriptstyle 1} \\ 1\ 5 \\ \times\quad 3 \\ \hline 4\ 5 \end{array}$$

Omar is 45 years old.

$45 - 20 = 25$

Omar is **25** years older than Henry.

Answer: **25 years older**

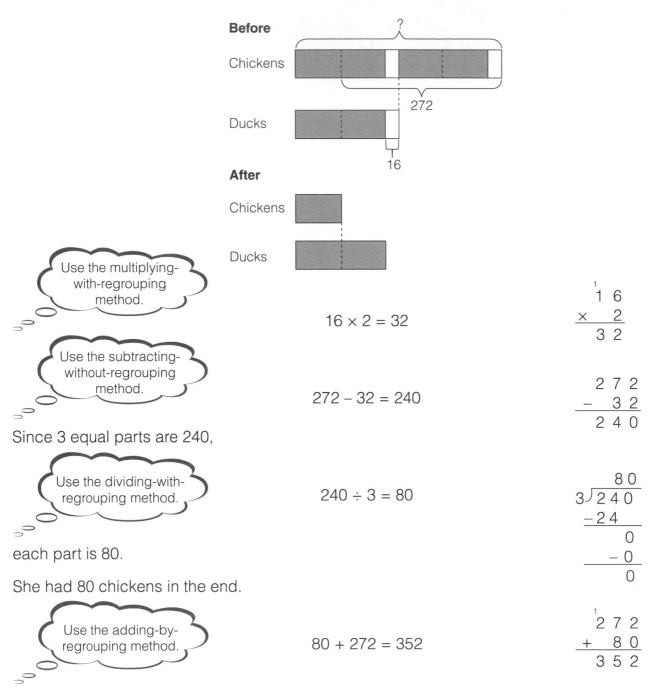

Before

Chickens

Ducks

272

16

After

Chickens

Ducks

Use the multiplying-with-regrouping method.

$$16 \times 2 = 32$$

$$\begin{array}{r} \overset{1}{1}\,6 \\ \times\ \ 2 \\ \hline 3\,2 \end{array}$$

Use the subtracting-without-regrouping method.

$$272 - 32 = 240$$

$$\begin{array}{r} 2\,7\,2 \\ -\ \ 3\,2 \\ \hline 2\,4\,0 \end{array}$$

Since 3 equal parts are 240,

Use the dividing-with-regrouping method.

$$240 \div 3 = 80$$

$$\begin{array}{r} 8\,0 \\ 3\overline{)2\,4\,0} \\ -2\,4 \\ \hline 0 \\ -\ 0 \\ \hline 0 \end{array}$$

each part is 80.

She had 80 chickens in the end.

Use the adding-by-regrouping method.

$$80 + 272 = 352$$

$$\begin{array}{r} \overset{1}{2}\,7\,2 \\ +\ \ 8\,0 \\ \hline 3\,5\,2 \end{array}$$

She had **352** chickens in the beginning.

Answer: **352 chickens**

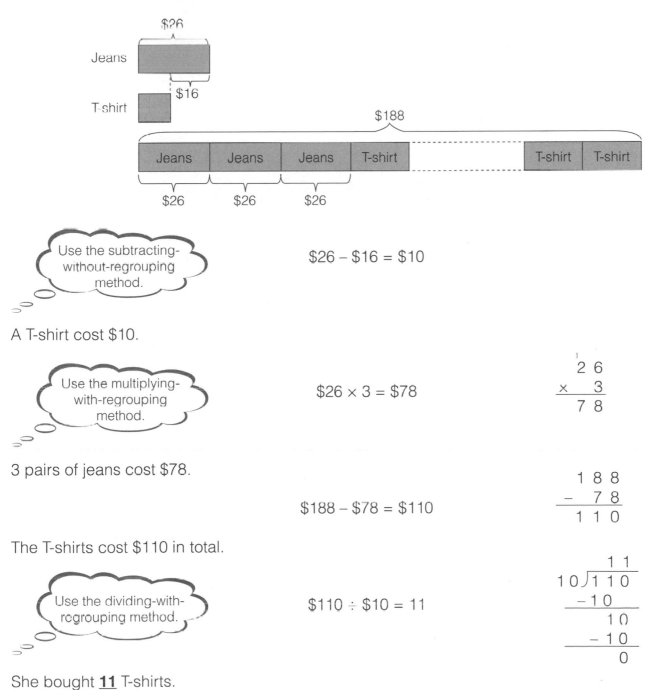

Use the subtracting-without-regrouping method.

$26 - $16 = $10

A T-shirt cost $10.

Use the multiplying-with-regrouping method.

$26 × 3 = $78

$$\begin{array}{r} \,\overset{1}{2}\,6 \\ \times\quad 3 \\ \hline 7\,8 \end{array}$$

3 pairs of jeans cost $78.

$188 - $78 = $110

$$\begin{array}{r} 1\,8\,8 \\ -\quad 7\,8 \\ \hline 1\,1\,0 \end{array}$$

The T-shirts cost $110 in total.

Use the dividing-with-regrouping method.

$110 ÷ $10 = 11

$$\begin{array}{r} 11 \\ 10\,\overline{)1\,1\,0} \\ -1\,0 \\ \hline 1\,0 \\ -1\,0 \\ \hline 0 \end{array}$$

She bought **11** T-shirts.

Answer: ___**11 T-shirts**___

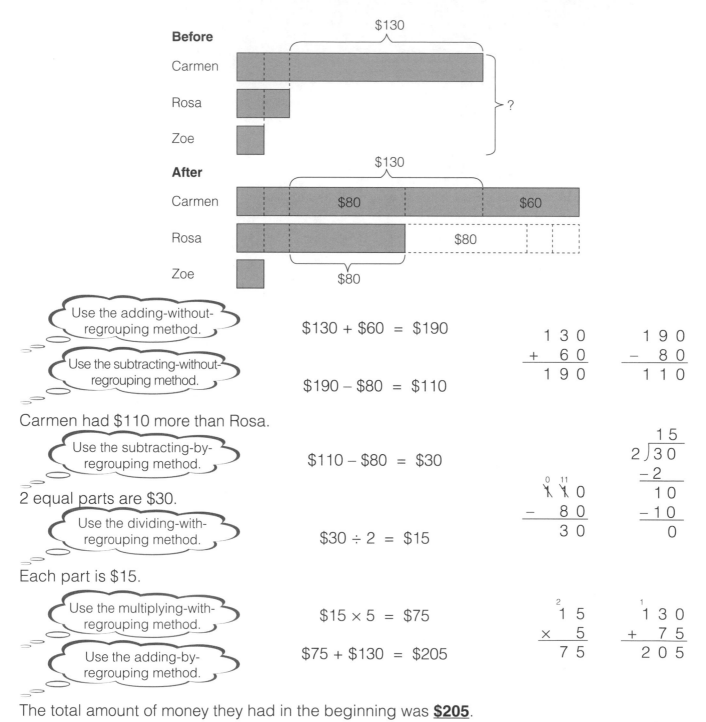

Before

$130

Carmen

Rosa

Zoe

?

After

$130

Carmen $80 $60

Rosa $80

Zoe $80

Use the adding-without-regrouping method.

$130 + $60 = $190

$$\begin{array}{r} 1\ 3\ 0 \\ +\ \ 6\ 0 \\ \hline 1\ 9\ 0 \end{array}$$

Use the subtracting-without-regrouping method.

$190 − $80 = $110

$$\begin{array}{r} 1\ 9\ 0 \\ -\ \ 8\ 0 \\ \hline 1\ 1\ 0 \end{array}$$

Carmen had $110 more than Rosa.

Use the subtracting-by-regrouping method.

$110 − $80 = $30

Use the dividing-with-regrouping method.

$30 ÷ 2 = $15

$$\begin{array}{r} 1\ 5 \\ 2\overline{)3\ 0} \\ -2 \\ \hline 1\ 0 \\ -1\ 0 \\ \hline 0 \end{array}$$

2 equal parts are $30.

Each part is $15.

Use the multiplying-with-regrouping method.

$15 × 5 = $75

$$\begin{array}{r} \overset{2}{1}\ 5 \\ \times\ \ \ 5 \\ \hline 7\ 5 \end{array}$$

Use the adding-by-regrouping method.

$75 + $130 = $205

$$\begin{array}{r} \overset{1}{1}\ 3\ 0 \\ +\ \ 7\ 5 \\ \hline 2\ 0\ 5 \end{array}$$

The total amount of money they had in the beginning was **$205**.

Answer: **$205**

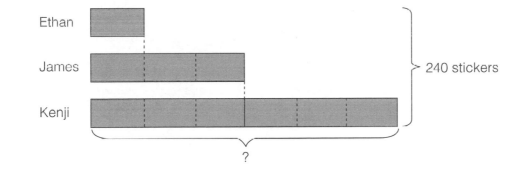

Since 10 equal parts are 240 stickers,

Use the dividing-with-regrouping method.

$240 \div 10 = 24$

```
        2 4
  10 ) 2 4 0
      - 2 0
        4 0
      - 4 0
          0
```

each part is 24.

Use the multiplying-with-regrouping method.

$24 \times 6 = 144$

```
      2
      2 4
   ×    6
    1 4 4
```

Kenji received **144** stickers.

Answer: **144 stickers**

Solution to Question 18

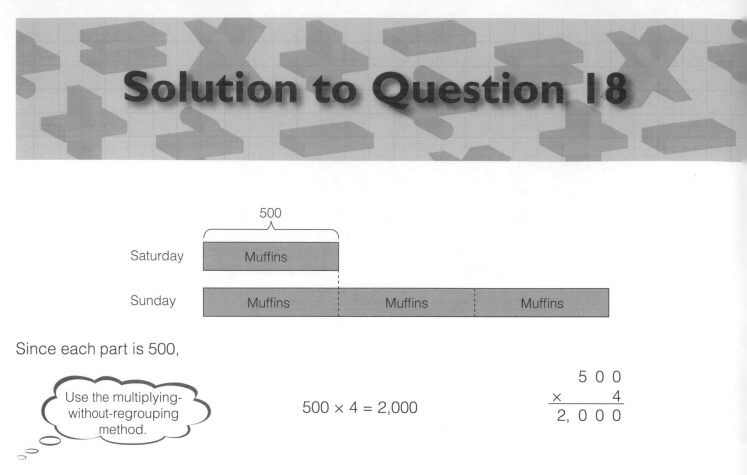

Since each part is 500,

> Use the multiplying-without-regrouping method.

$$500 \times 4 = 2,000$$

$$\begin{array}{r} 5\,0\,0 \\ \times \quad\quad 4 \\ \hline 2,\,0\,0\,0 \end{array}$$

4 equal parts are 2,000.

Mrs. Rothberg baked 2,000 muffins on both days.

She sold them in groups of 5.

> Use the dividing-with-regrouping method.

$$2,000 \div 5 = 400$$

$$\begin{array}{r} 4\,0\,0 \\ 5\overline{)2,\,0\,0\,0} \\ -2\,0 \\ \hline 0 \\ -\,0 \\ \hline 0 \\ -\,0 \\ \hline 0 \end{array}$$

She sold 400 groups of 5 muffins.

$$400 \times \$4 = \$1,600$$

$$\begin{array}{r} 4\,0\,0 \\ \times \quad\quad 4 \\ \hline 1,\,6\,0\,0 \end{array}$$

She would earn **$1,600** by selling all her muffins on both days.

Answer: _____ **$1,600**

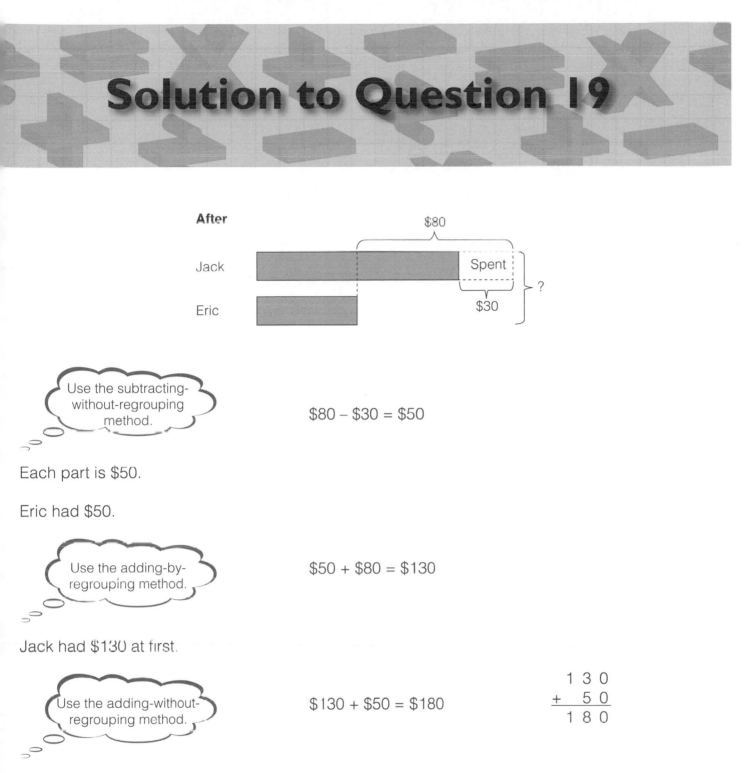

After

Jack

Eric

$80

Spent

$30

?

> Use the subtracting-without-regrouping method.

$80 – $30 = $50

Each part is $50.

Eric had $50.

> Use the adding-by-regrouping method.

$50 + $80 = $130

Jack had $130 at first.

> Use the adding-without-regrouping method.

$130 + $50 = $180

```
  1 3 0
+   5 0
  1 8 0
```

The boys had **$180** altogether in the beginning.

Answer: **$180**

1 shirt cost $15 more than a pair of shorts.

Use the multiplying-with-regrouping method.

$15 × 3 = $45

$$\begin{array}{r} {}^{1} \\ 1\ 5 \\ \times \quad 3 \\ \hline 4\ 5 \end{array}$$

Shirt

A pair of shorts

$15

3 shirts cost $45 more than a pair of shorts.

$101

Shorts	Shorts	Shorts	Shorts	Shorts	Shirt	Shirt	Shirt	$45

Use the subtracting-by-regrouping-twice method.

$101 − $45 = $56

$$\begin{array}{r} {}^{0}{}^{9}{}^{11} \\ 1\ 0\ 1 \\ -\quad 4\ 5 \\ \hline 5\ 6 \end{array}$$

Since 8 equal parts are $56,

Use the dividing-without-regrouping method.

$56 ÷ 8 = $7

8 × 7 = 56

each part is $7.

Each pair of shorts cost $7.

Use the adding-by-regrouping method.

$15 + $7 = $22

Each shirt cost **$22**.

Answer: ___**$22**___

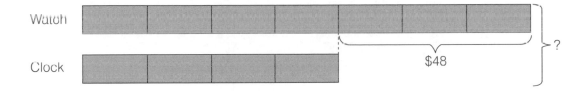

Since 3 equal parts are $48,

Use the dividing-with-regrouping method.

$48 ÷ 3 = $16

```
      1 6
   3 ⟌ 4 8
     - 3
     ───
       1 8
     - 1 8
     ─────
         0
```

each part is $16.

There are 11 parts in total.

Use the multiplying-with-regrouping method.

$16 × 11 = $176

```
      1 6
    × 1 1
    ─────
      1 6
  + 1 6
  ───────
    1 7 6
```

The total cost of the 2 items is **$176**.

Answer: __**$176**__

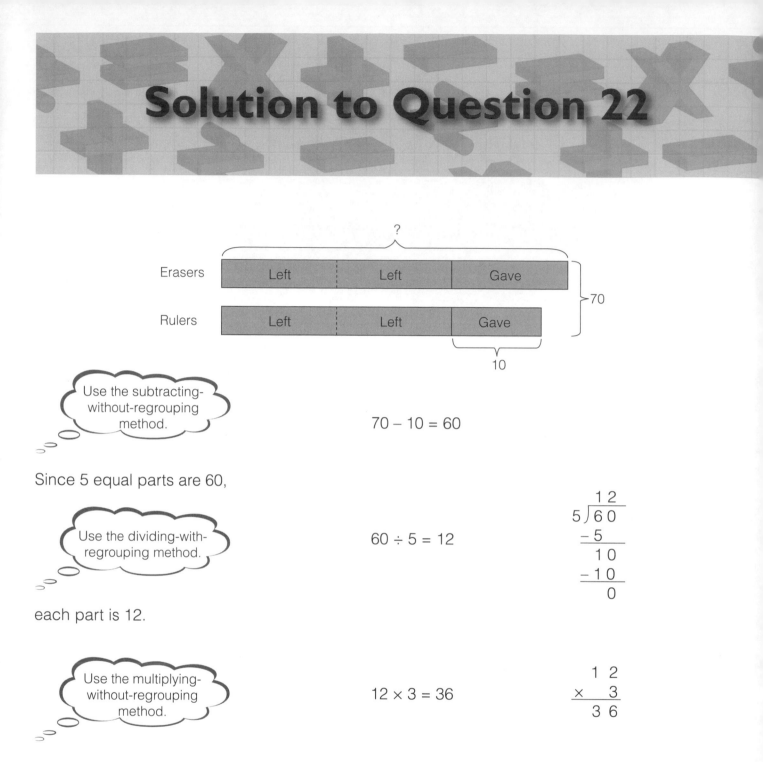

70 − 10 = 60

Since 5 equal parts are 60,

60 ÷ 5 = 12

each part is 12.

12 × 3 = 36

He had **36** erasers in the beginning.

Answer: **36 erasers**

Solution to Question 23

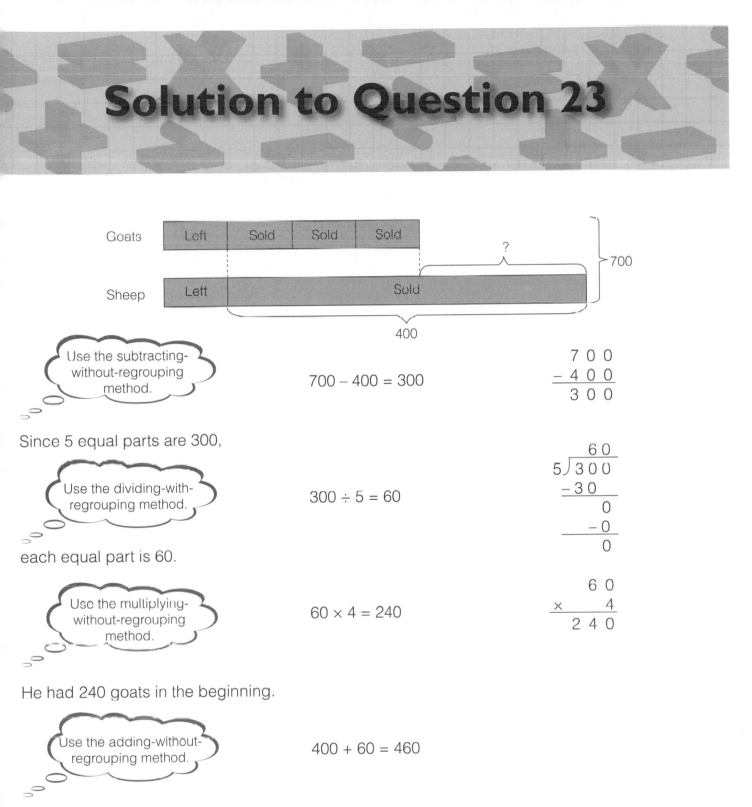

Goats: Left | Sold | Sold | Sold ? 700

Sheep: Left | Sold 400

Use the subtracting-without-regrouping method.

$$700 - 400 = 300$$

$$\begin{array}{r} 700 \\ -\ 400 \\ \hline 300 \end{array}$$

Since 5 equal parts are 300,

Use the dividing-with-regrouping method.

$$300 \div 5 = 60$$

$$\begin{array}{r} 60 \\ 5\overline{)300} \\ -30 \\ \hline 0 \\ -\ 0 \\ \hline 0 \end{array}$$

each equal part is 60.

Use the multiplying-without-regrouping method.

$$60 \times 4 = 240$$

$$\begin{array}{r} 60 \\ \times\quad 4 \\ \hline 240 \end{array}$$

He had 240 goats in the beginning.

Use the adding-without-regrouping method.

$$400 + 60 = 460$$

He had 460 sheep in the beginning.

$$460 - 240 = 220$$

He had **220** more sheep than goats in the beginning.

Answer: __220 more sheep__

Solution to Question 24

Convert $3\frac{2}{3}$ into a mixed number.

$$3\frac{2}{3} = \frac{11}{3}$$

There are 11 equal parts for female workers and 3 equal parts for male workers.

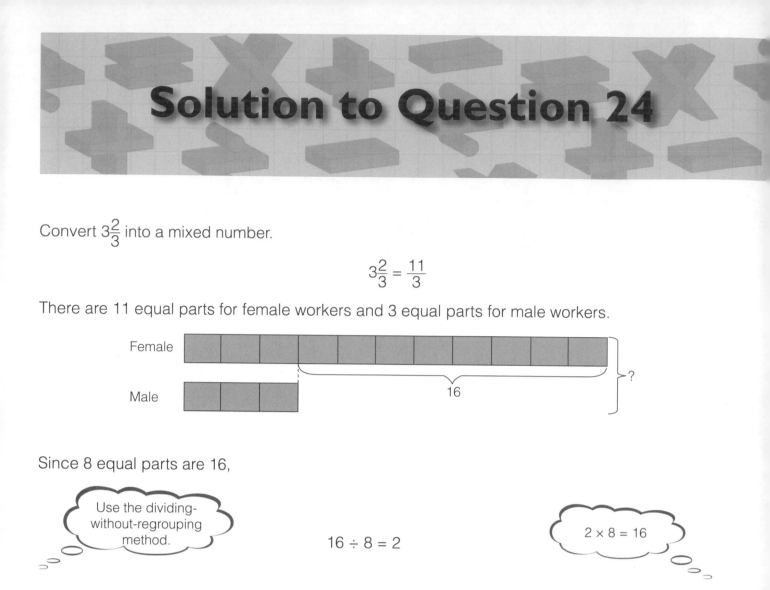

Since 8 equal parts are 16,

Use the dividing-without-regrouping method.

$$16 \div 8 = 2$$

$$2 \times 8 = 16$$

each part is 2.

There are 14 equal parts altogether.

Use the multiplying-without-regrouping method.

$$2 \times 14 = 28$$

$$\begin{array}{r} 1\ 4 \\ \times\quad 2 \\ \hline 2\ 8 \end{array}$$

The total number of workers in the factory is **28**.

Answer: **28 workers**

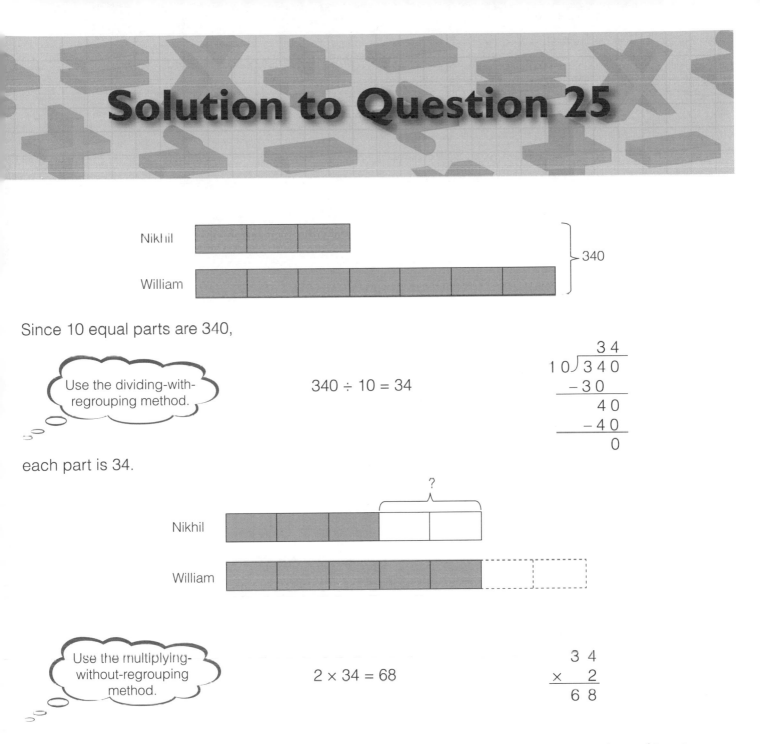

Since 10 equal parts are 340,

Use the dividing-with-regrouping method.

$$340 \div 10 = 34$$

each part is 34.

Use the multiplying-without-regrouping method.

$$2 \times 34 = 68$$

William must give Nikhil **68** books so that each of them would have the same number of books.

Answer: __**68 books**__

1 chicken cost $5 more than a duck.

Use the multiplying-without-regrouping method.

$5 × 5 = $25

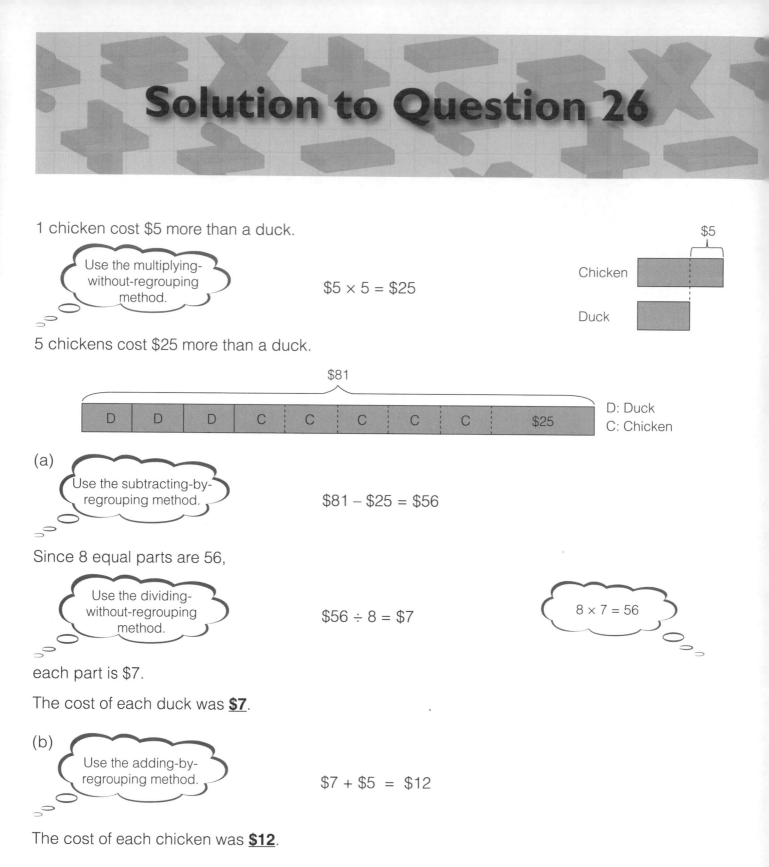

Chicken

$5

Duck

5 chickens cost $25 more than a duck.

$81

| D | D | D | C | C | C | C | C | $25 |

D: Duck
C: Chicken

(a)

Use the subtracting-by-regrouping method.

$81 − $25 = $56

Since 8 equal parts are 56,

Use the dividing-without-regrouping method.

$56 ÷ 8 = $7

8 × 7 = 56

each part is $7.

The cost of each duck was **$7**.

(b)

Use the adding-by-regrouping method.

$7 + $5 = $12

The cost of each chicken was **$12**.

Answer: (a) _____ **$7** _____

(b) _____ **$12** _____

Solution to Question 27

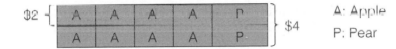

A: Apple
P: Pear

8 apples and 2 pears cost $4, so 4 apples and 1 pear cost $2.

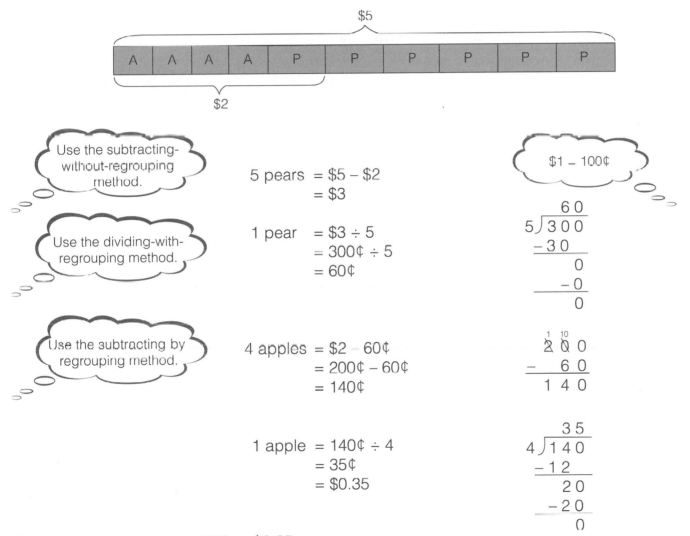

Use the subtracting-without-regrouping method.

5 pears = $5 − $2
= $3

Use the dividing-with-regrouping method.

1 pear = $3 ÷ 5
= 300¢ ÷ 5
= 60¢

$1 − 100¢

```
  6 0
5 ) 3 0 0
  − 3 0
      0
    − 0
      0
```

Use the subtracting by regrouping method.

4 apples = $2 − 60¢
= 200¢ − 60¢
= 140¢

```
  1 10
  2 0̶ 0
−   6 0
  1 4 0
```

1 apple = 140¢ ÷ 4
= 35¢
= $0.35

```
    3 5
4 ) 1 4 0
  − 1 2
      2 0
    − 2 0
        0
```

The price of an apple was **35¢** or **$0.35**.

Answer: **35¢ or $0.35**

Add 4 to the divisor, 7, so that the number will have a remainder of 4 when divided by 7.

Use the adding-by-regrouping method.

$7 + 4 = 11$

Numbers that have a remainder of 4 when divided by 7:

+ 7 + 7 ...

11, 18, 25, 32, 39, 46, 53, 60, 67, 74, 81, **88**, 95

Add 8 to the divisor, 10, so that the number will have a remainder of 8 when divided by 10.

Use the adding-without-regrouping method.

$10 + 8 = 18$

Numbers that have a remainder of 8 when divided by 10:

+ 10 + 10 ...

18, 28, 38, 48, 58, 68, 78, **88**, 98

Use the common-multiple method.

Since 88 is common in both lists and the number is more than 50 but less than 100, the number must be **88**.

Answer: _____**88**_____

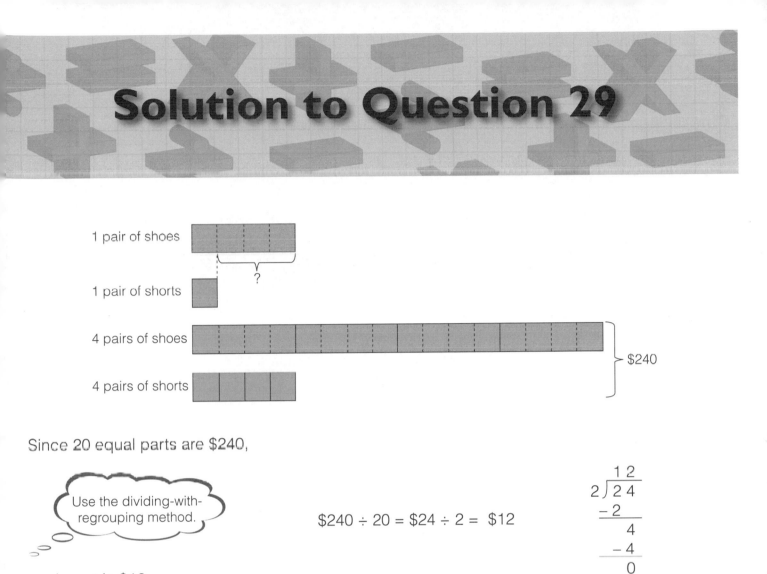

Since 20 equal parts are $240,

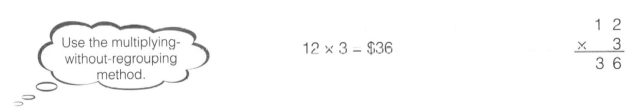

Use the dividing-with-regrouping method.

$$\$240 \div 20 = \$24 \div 2 = \$12$$

$$\begin{array}{r} 1\,2 \\ 2\overline{)2\,4} \\ -2 \\ \hline 4 \\ -4 \\ \hline 0 \end{array}$$

each part is $12.

Use the multiplying-without-regrouping method.

$$12 \times 3 - \$36$$

$$\begin{array}{r} 1\,2 \\ \times\quad 3 \\ \hline 3\,6 \end{array}$$

The difference in price between a pair of shoes and a pair of shorts was **$36**.

Answer: **$36**

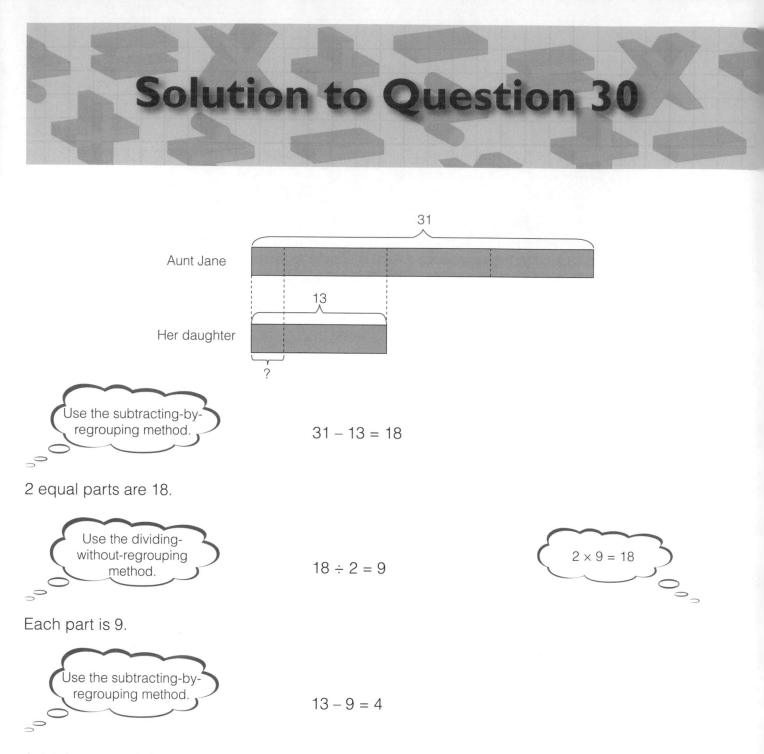

31 − 13 = 18

2 equal parts are 18.

18 ÷ 2 = 9

2 × 9 = 18

Each part is 9.

13 − 9 = 4

Aunt Jane was 3 times as old as her daughter **4** years ago.

Answer: __**4 years ago**__

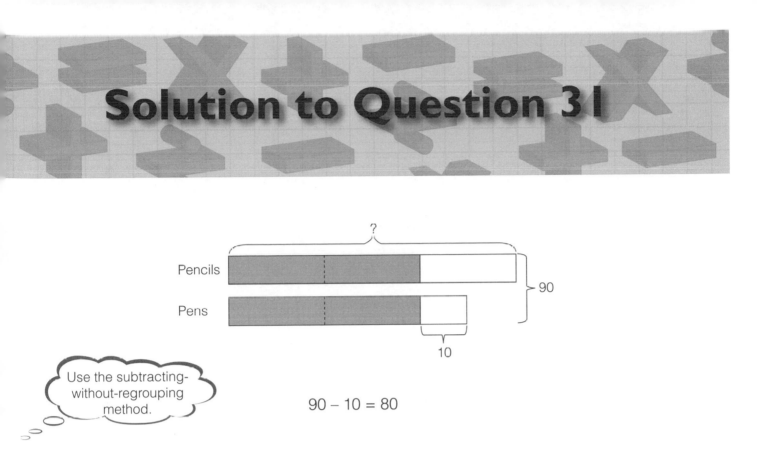

Use the subtracting-without-regrouping method.

$$90 - 10 = 80$$

Since 5 equal parts are 80,

Use the dividing-with-regrouping method.

$$80 \div 5 = 16$$

```
      1 6
  5 ) 8 0
     -5
      3 0
     -3 0
        0
```

each part is 16.

Number of pencils he had in the beginning = 3 parts

Use the multiplying-with-regrouping method.

$$16 \times 3 = 48$$

```
     ¹
    1 6
  ×   3
  ─────
    4 8
```

He had **48** pencils in the beginning.

Answer: ___**48 pencils**___

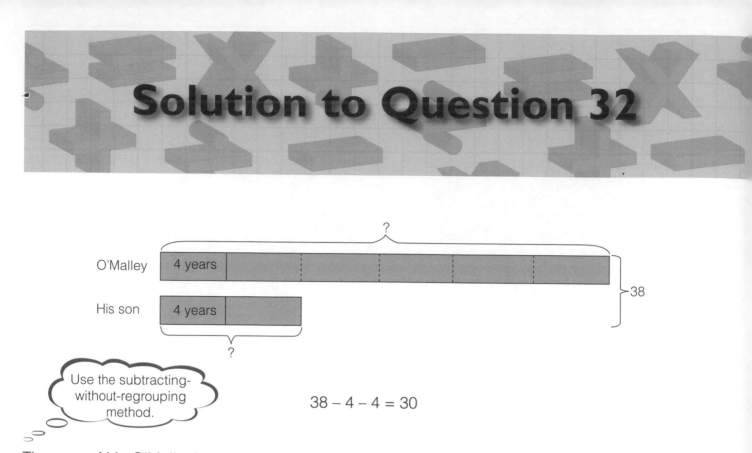

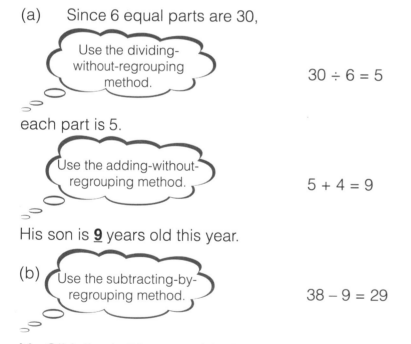

$$38 - 4 - 4 = 30$$

The sum of Mr. O'Malley's age and his son's age was 30 years four years ago.

(a)   Since 6 equal parts are 30,

Use the dividing-without-regrouping method.

$$30 ÷ 6 = 5$$

$$6 × 5 = 30$$

each part is 5.

Use the adding-without-regrouping method.

$$5 + 4 = 9$$

His son is **9** years old this year.

(b) Use the subtracting-by-regrouping method.

$$38 - 9 = 29$$

Mr. O'Malley is **29** years old this year.

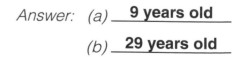

Answer: (a) __9 years old__

(b) __29 years old__

Solution to Question 33

Add 3 years each to Albert's age and his grandfather's age,

> Use the adding-with-regrouping method.

$$64 + 3 + 3 = 70$$

their total age will be 70 years in 3 years.

In 3 years

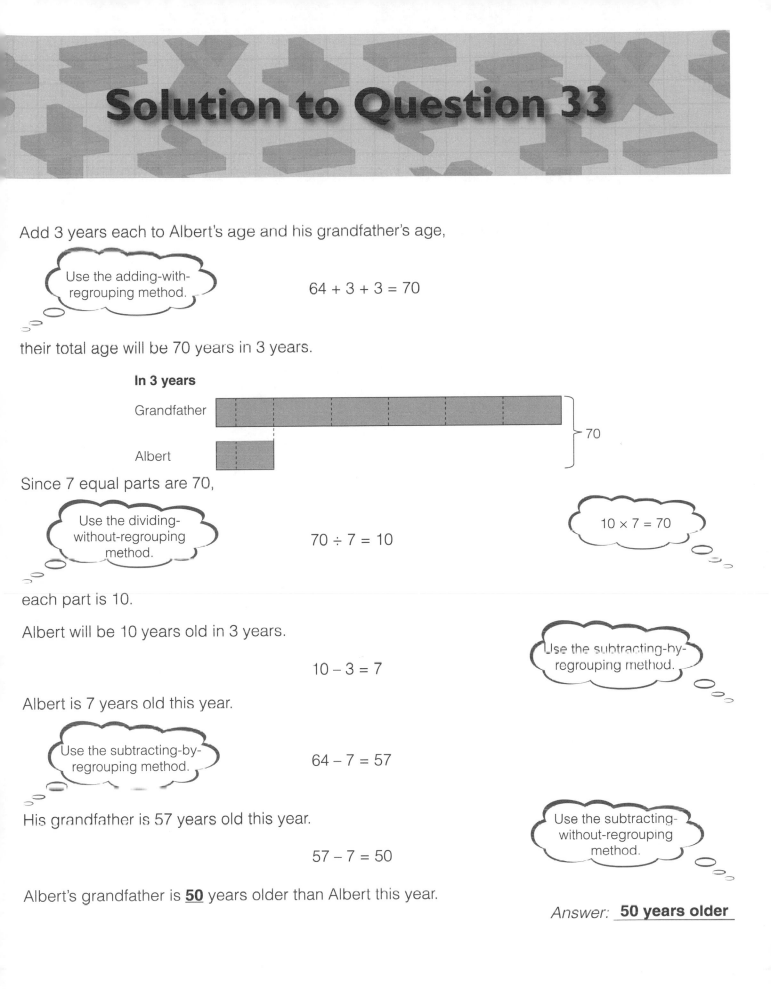

Grandfather

Albert

} 70

Since 7 equal parts are 70,

> Use the dividing-without-regrouping method.

$$70 \div 7 = 10$$

> $10 \times 7 = 70$

each part is 10.

Albert will be 10 years old in 3 years.

$$10 - 3 = 7$$

> Use the subtracting-by-regrouping method.

Albert is 7 years old this year.

> Use the subtracting-by-regrouping method.

$$64 - 7 = 57$$

His grandfather is 57 years old this year.

$$57 - 7 = 50$$

> Use the subtracting-without-regrouping method.

Albert's grandfather is **50** years older than Albert this year.

Answer: __**50 years older**__

Add 3 to the divisor, 4, so that the number will have a remainder of 3 when divided by 4.

Use the adding-without-regrouping method.

$$4 + 3 = 7$$

Numbers that have a remainder of 3 when divided by 4

+ 4 + 4 ...

7, 11, 15, 19, 23, 27, 31, 35, 39, 43, 47, 51, 55, 59, 63, 67, **71**, 75, 79

Add 1 to the divisor, 7, so that the number will have a remainder of 1 when divided by 7.

Use the adding-without-regrouping method.

$$7 + 1 = 8$$

Numbers that have a remainder of 1 when divided by 7

+ 7 + 7 ...

8, 15, 22, 29, 36, 43, 50, 57, 64, **71**, 78

Use the common-multiple method.

Since 71 is common in both lists and the number is between 60 and 80, the number must be **71**.

Answer: _____ **71**

Add 1 to the divisor, 3, so that the number will have a remainder of 1 when divided by 3.

> Use the adding-without-regrouping method.

$$3 + 1 = 4$$

Numbers that have a remainder of 1 when divided by 3

+ 3 + 3 ...
4, 7, 10, 13, 16, 19, 22, 25, 28, 31, 34, 37, 40, 43, 46, 49, 52, 55, **58**

Add 2 to the divisor, 4, so that the number will have a remainder of 2 when divided by 4.

> Use the adding-without-regrouping method.

$$4 + 2 = 6$$

Numbers that have a remainder of 2 when divided by 4

4   4 ...
6, 10, 14, 18, 22, 26, 30, 34, 38, 42, 46, 50, 54, **58**

> Use the common-multiple method.

Since 58 is common in both lists and the number is between 50 and 60, the number must be **58**.

Answer: **58**

$$1 - \frac{4}{9} = \frac{9}{9} - \frac{4}{9} = \frac{5}{9}$$

Her remaining money was $\frac{5}{9}$.

Since $\frac{1}{3}$ of her remaining money was spent on rent,

$$\frac{2}{3} = \$180 + \$270 + \$50.$$

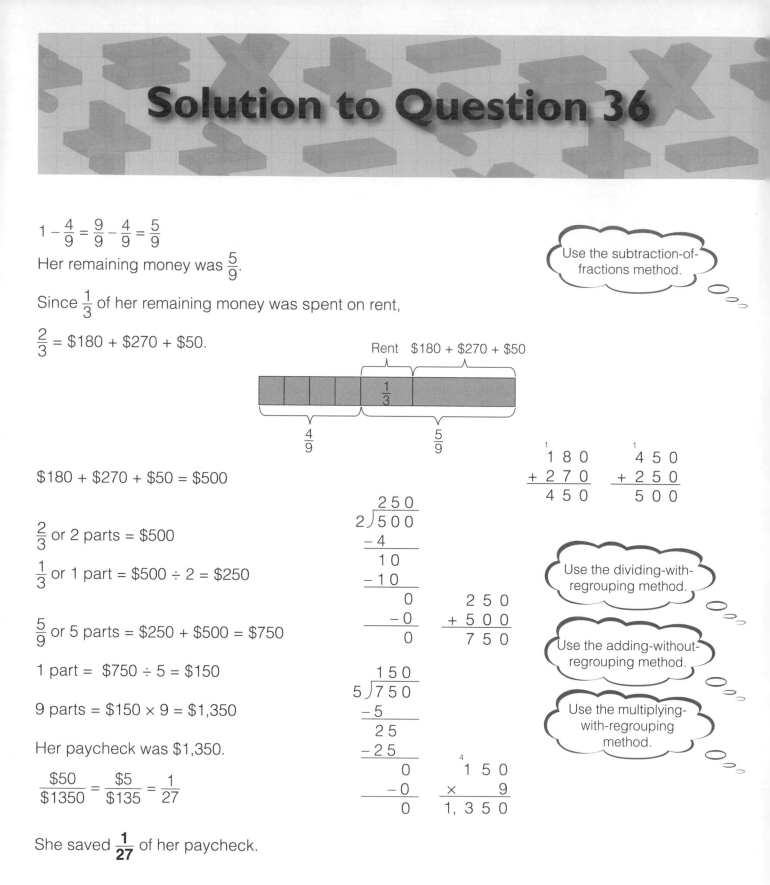

Rent $180 + $270 + $50

$$\frac{4}{9} \qquad \frac{5}{9}$$

$$\begin{array}{r} {}^{1}\ 1\ 8\ 0 \\ +\ 2\ 7\ 0 \\ \hline 4\ 5\ 0 \end{array} \qquad \begin{array}{r} {}^{1}\ 4\ 5\ 0 \\ +\ 2\ 5\ 0 \\ \hline 5\ 0\ 0 \end{array}$$

$180 + $270 + $50 = $500

$\frac{2}{3}$ or 2 parts = $500

$\frac{1}{3}$ or 1 part = $500 ÷ 2 = $250

$$\begin{array}{r} 250 \\ 2\overline{)500} \\ -4 \\ \hline 10 \\ -10 \\ \hline 0 \\ -0 \\ \hline 0 \end{array}$$

$\frac{5}{9}$ or 5 parts = $250 + $500 = $750

$$\begin{array}{r} 250 \\ +\ 500 \\ \hline 750 \end{array}$$

1 part = $750 ÷ 5 = $150

$$\begin{array}{r} 150 \\ 5\overline{)750} \\ -5 \\ \hline 25 \\ -25 \\ \hline 0 \\ -0 \\ \hline 0 \end{array}$$

9 parts = $150 × 9 = $1,350

Her paycheck was $1,350.

$$\frac{\$50}{\$1350} = \frac{\$5}{\$135} = \frac{1}{27}$$

$$\begin{array}{r} {}^{4}\ 1\ 5\ 0 \\ \times 9 \\ \hline 1,\ 3\ 5\ 0 \end{array}$$

She saved $\frac{1}{27}$ of her paycheck.

Use the subtraction-of-fractions method.

Use the dividing-with-regrouping method.

Use the adding-without-regrouping method.

Use the multiplying-with-regrouping method.

Answer: _____ $\frac{1}{27}$ _____

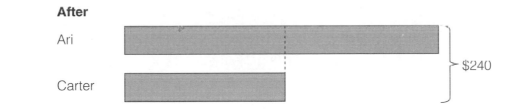

After

Ari

Carter

$240

Since 3 equal parts are $240,

Use the dividing-with-regrouping method.

$240 ÷ 3 = $80

```
        8 0
   3 ) 2 4 0
     - 2 4
         0
       - 0
         0
```

each part is $80.

Carter had $80 after giving Ari $16.

Use the adding-without-regrouping method.

$80 + $16 = $96

Carter had $96 in the beginning.

Use the subtracting-by-regrouping-twice method.

$240 − $96 = $144

```
   1  13  10
   2   4   0
   −      9  6
       1  4  4
```

Ari had $144 in the beginning.

$144 − $96 = $48

```
   0  13  14
   1   4   4
       9   6
       4   8
```

Ari had **$48** more than Carter in the beginning.

Answer: _____ **$48**

8 shirts and 5 pants = $695

3 shirts and 3 pants = $300

Using the lowest common multiple of 3 and 5 to obtain the same number of pants,

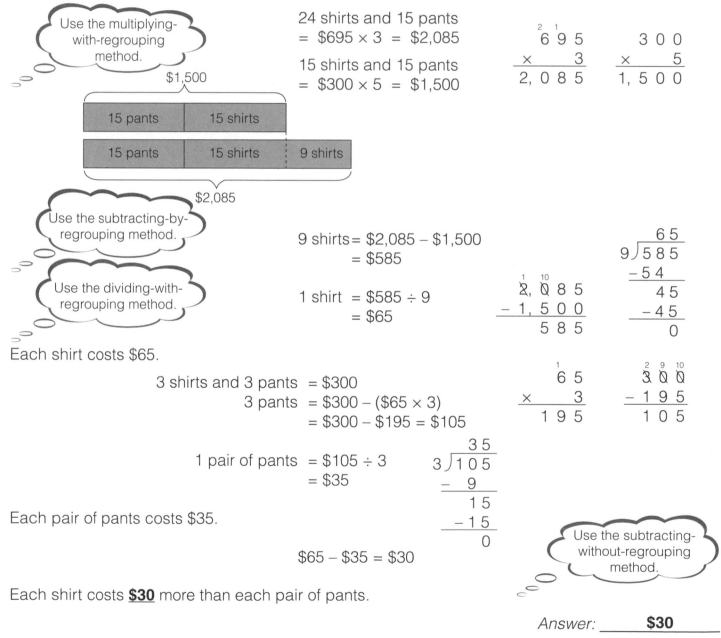

Use the multiplying-with-regrouping method.

24 shirts and 15 pants
= $695 × 3 = $2,085

15 shirts and 15 pants
= $300 × 5 = $1,500

$$\begin{array}{r} {}^{2}{}^{1} \\ 6\,9\,5 \\ \times\quad 3 \\ \hline 2,0\,8\,5 \end{array} \qquad \begin{array}{r} 3\,0\,0 \\ \times\quad 5 \\ \hline 1,5\,0\,0 \end{array}$$

$1,500

| 15 pants | 15 shirts |

| 15 pants | 15 shirts | 9 shirts |

$2,085

Use the subtracting-by-regrouping method.

9 shirts = $2,085 − $1,500
= $585

$$9\overline{)585} \\ \,6\,5 \\ -5\,4 \\ \hline 4\,5 \\ -4\,5 \\ \hline \ \ 0$$

Use the dividing-with-regrouping method.

1 shirt = $585 ÷ 9
= $65

$$\begin{array}{r} {}^{1}\ {}^{10} \\ 2,\cancel{0}\,8\,5 \\ -1,5\,0\,0 \\ \hline 5\,8\,5 \end{array}$$

Each shirt costs $65.

3 shirts and 3 pants = $300

3 pants = $300 − ($65 × 3)
= $300 − $195 = $105

$$\begin{array}{r} {}^{1} \\ 6\,5 \\ \times\ 3 \\ \hline 1\,9\,5 \end{array} \qquad \begin{array}{r} {}^{2}\ {}^{9}\ {}^{10} \\ \cancel{3}\,\cancel{0}\,\cancel{0} \\ -1\,9\,5 \\ \hline 1\,0\,5 \end{array}$$

1 pair of pants = $105 ÷ 3
= $35

$$3\overline{)105} \\ \,3\,5 \\ -\ 9 \\ \hline 1\,5 \\ -1\,5 \\ \hline \ \ 0$$

Each pair of pants costs $35.

$65 − $35 = $30

Use the subtracting-without-regrouping method.

Each shirt costs **$30** more than each pair of pants.

Answer: **$30**

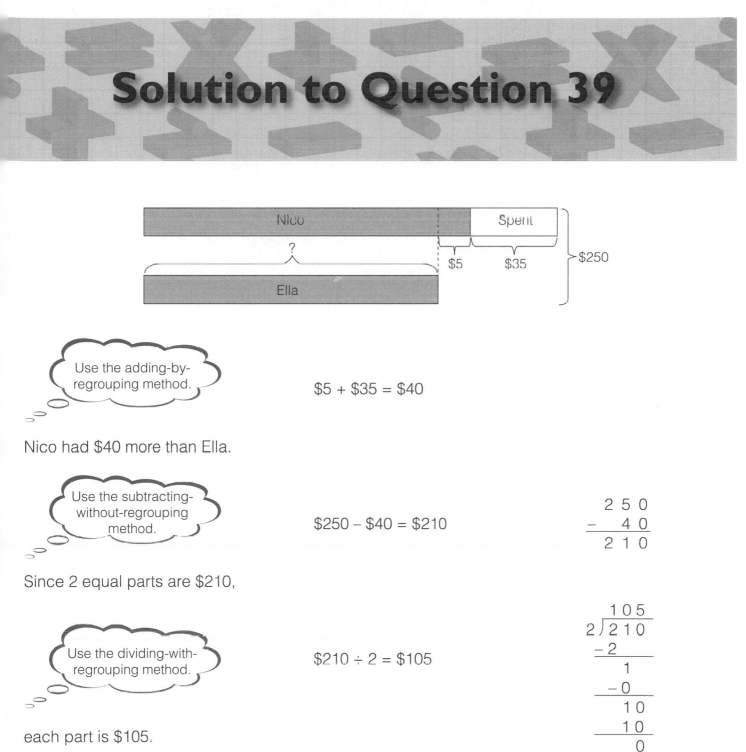

Use the adding-by-regrouping method.

$5 + $35 = $40

Nico had $40 more than Ella.

Use the subtracting-without-regrouping method.

$250 − $40 = $210

```
  2 5 0
−   4 0
  2 1 0
```

Since 2 equal parts are $210,

Use the dividing-with-regrouping method.

$210 ÷ 2 = $105

```
      1 0 5
  2 ) 2 1 0
     −2
      1
     − 0
       1 0
       1 0
        0
```

each part is $105.

Ella had **$105**.

Answer: ____**$105**____

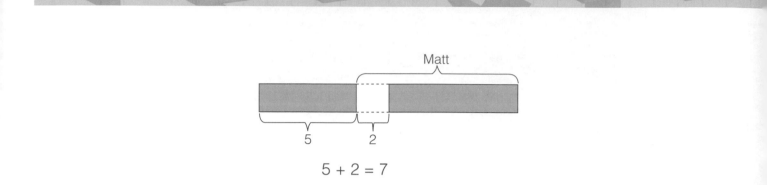

$$5 + 2 = 7$$

Half of the remaining marbles was 7.

> Use the adding-without-regrouping method.

$$7 + 2 = 9$$

Matt received 9 marbles.

$$5 + 9 + 1 = 15$$

> Use the adding-by-regrouping method.

Half of Manuel's marbles was 15.

$$15 + 1 = 16$$

Lily received 16 marbles.

$$5 + 9 + 16 = 30$$

Manuel had **30** marbles in the beginning.

Answer: __**30 marbles**__

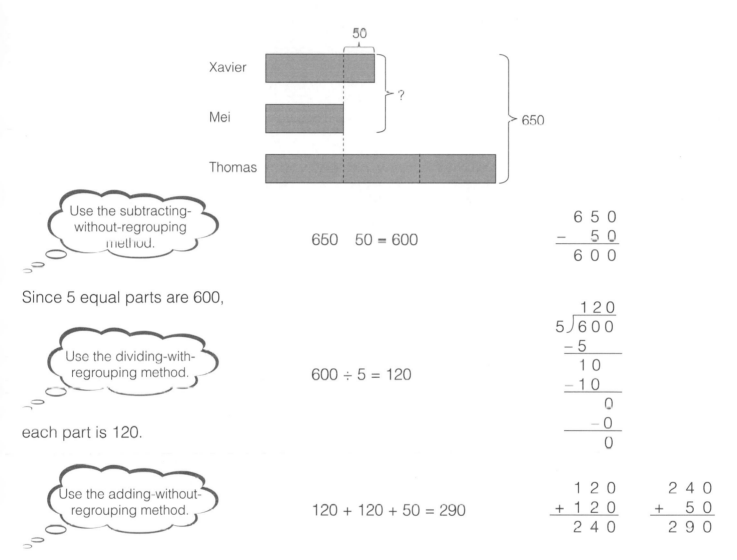

Use the subtracting-without-regrouping method.

$$650 - 50 = 600$$

$$\begin{array}{r} 6\ 5\ 0 \\ -\ \ \ 5\ 0 \\ \hline 6\ 0\ 0 \end{array}$$

Since 5 equal parts are 600,

Use the dividing-with-regrouping method.

$$600 \div 5 = 120$$

$$\begin{array}{r} 1\ 2\ 0 \\ 5\overline{)6\ 0\ 0} \\ -5 \\ \hline 1\ 0 \\ -1\ 0 \\ \hline 0 \\ -\ 0 \\ \hline 0 \end{array}$$

each part is 120.

Use the adding-without-regrouping method.

$$120 + 120 + 50 = 290$$

$$\begin{array}{r} 1\ 2\ 0 \\ +\ 1\ 2\ 0 \\ \hline 2\ 4\ 0 \end{array} \qquad \begin{array}{r} 2\ 4\ 0 \\ +\ \ \ 5\ 0 \\ \hline 2\ 9\ 0 \end{array}$$

Xavier and Mei had **290** marbles altogether.

Answer: **290 marbles**

At first

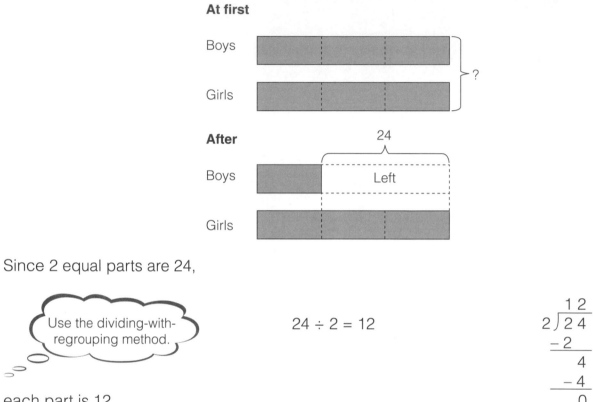

Since 2 equal parts are 24,

Use the dividing-with-regrouping method.

$24 \div 2 = 12$

$$\begin{array}{r} 1\,2 \\ 2\overline{)\,2\,4} \\ -2 \\ \hline 4 \\ -4 \\ \hline 0 \end{array}$$

each part is 12.

Use the multiplying-with-regrouping method.

$12 \times 6 = 72$

$$\begin{array}{r} {}^{1} \\ 1\,2 \\ \times\ \ 6 \\ \hline 7\,2 \end{array}$$

There were **72** children in the beginning.

Answer: __**72 children**__

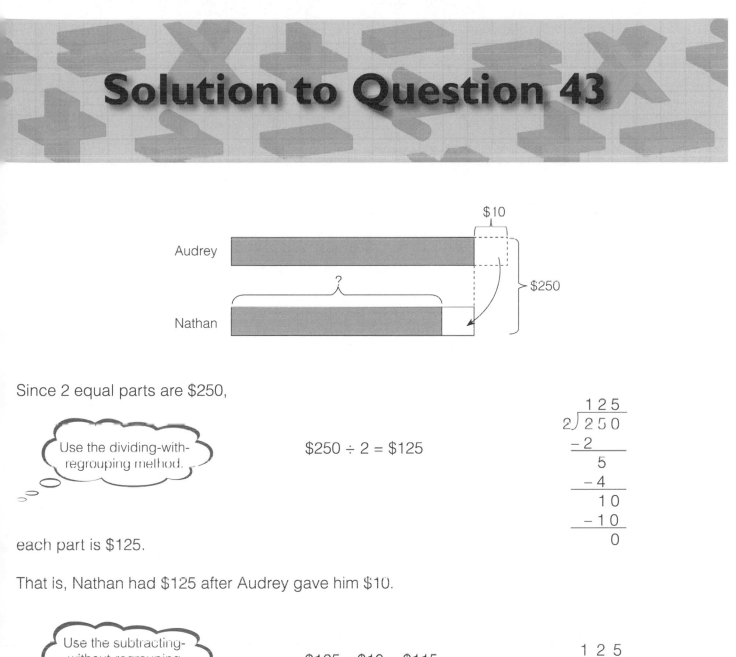

Since 2 equal parts are $250,

Use the dividing-with-regrouping method.

$250 ÷ 2 = $125

```
    1 2 5
2 ) 2 5 0
   -2
    ───
    5
   -4
    ───
    1 0
   -1 0
    ───
    0
```

each part is $125.

That is, Nathan had $125 after Audrey gave him $10.

Use the subtracting-without-regrouping method.

$125 – $10 = $115

```
  1 2 5
-   1 0
  ─────
  1 1 5
```

Nathan had **$115** in the beginning.

Answer: _____ **$115**

Solution to Question 44

Use the multiplying-with-regrouping method.

4 waffles + 4 pancakes = $18

8 waffles + 8 pancakes = $18 × 2
$$= \$36$$

$$\begin{array}{r} {\scriptstyle 1} \\ 1\,8 \\ \times \quad 2 \\ \hline 3\,6 \end{array}$$

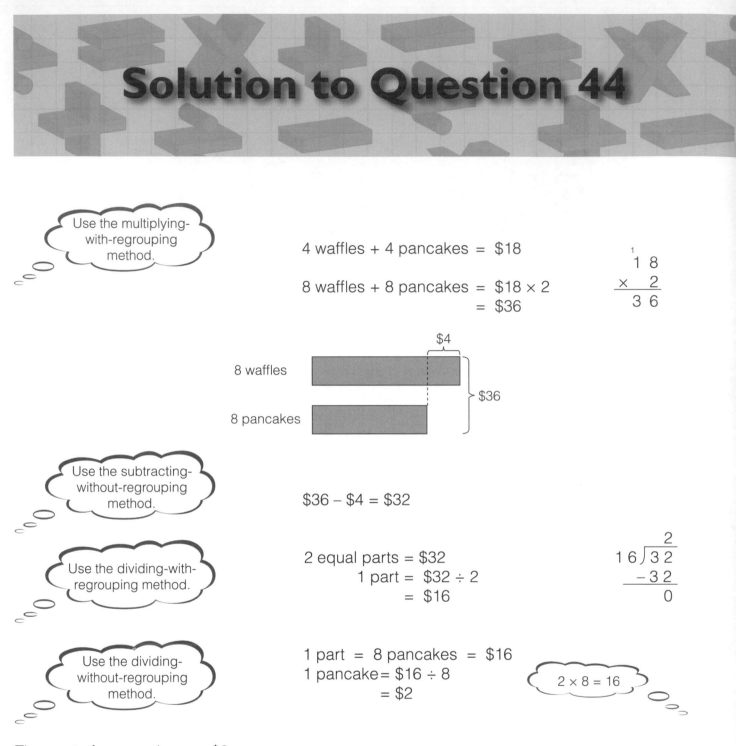

Use the subtracting-without-regrouping method.

$36 – $4 = $32

Use the dividing-with-regrouping method.

2 equal parts = $32
  1 part = $32 ÷ 2
         = $16

$$\begin{array}{r} 2 \\ 16\,\overline{)\,3\,2} \\ -3\,2 \\ \hline 0 \end{array}$$

Use the dividing-without-regrouping method.

1 part = 8 pancakes = $16
1 pancake = $16 ÷ 8
          = $2

2 × 8 = 16

The cost of a pancake was **$2**.

Answer: _____**$2**

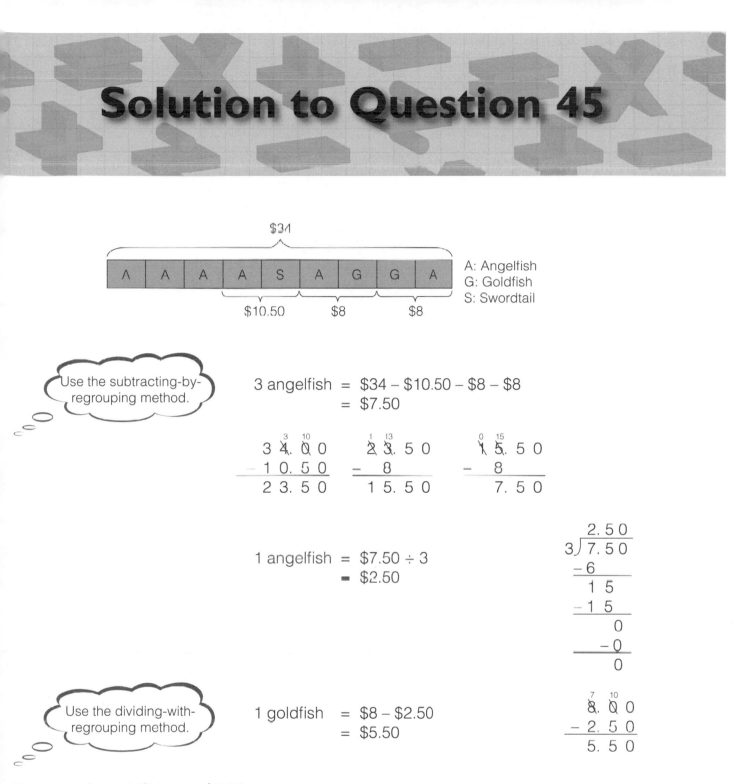

$34

A: Angelfish
G: Goldfish
S: Swordtail

$10.50 $8 $8

Use the subtracting-by-regrouping method.

3 angelfish = $34 − $10.50 − $8 − $8
            = $7.50

$$
\begin{array}{r}
\overset{3}{}\overset{10}{}\\
3\ 4.\ 0\ 0\\
-\ 1\ 0.\ 5\ 0\\
\hline
2\ 3.\ 5\ 0
\end{array}
\qquad
\begin{array}{r}
\overset{1}{}\overset{13}{}\\
2\ 3.\ 5\ 0\\
-\ \ \ \ 8\\
\hline
1\ 5.\ 5\ 0
\end{array}
\qquad
\begin{array}{r}
\overset{0}{}\overset{15}{}\\
1\ 5.\ 5\ 0\\
-\ \ \ \ 8\\
\hline
7.\ 5\ 0
\end{array}
$$

1 angelfish = $7.50 ÷ 3
            = $2.50

$$
\begin{array}{r}
2.\ 5\ 0\\
3\overline{)7.\ 5\ 0}\\
-6\\
\hline
1\ 5\\
-1\ 5\\
\hline
0\\
-0\\
\hline
0
\end{array}
$$

Use the dividing-with-regrouping method.

1 goldfish = $8 − $2.50
           = $5.50

$$
\begin{array}{r}
\overset{7}{}\overset{10}{}\\
8.\ 0\ 0\\
-\ 2.\ 5\ 0\\
\hline
5.\ 5\ 0
\end{array}
$$

The cost of a goldfish was **$5.50**.

Answer: _____ **$5.50**

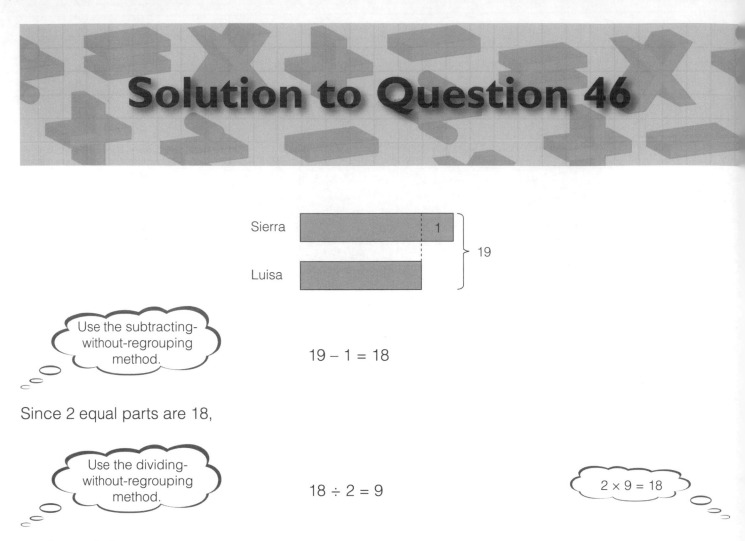

19 − 1 = 18

Since 2 equal parts are 18,

18 ÷ 2 = 9

2 × 9 = 18

each part is 9.

Luisa had 9 stamps after Sierra gave her 2 stamps.

9 − 2 = 7

Luisa had 7 stamps in the beginning.

19 − 7 = 12

Sierra had **12** stamps in the beginning.

Answer: ___**12 stamps**___

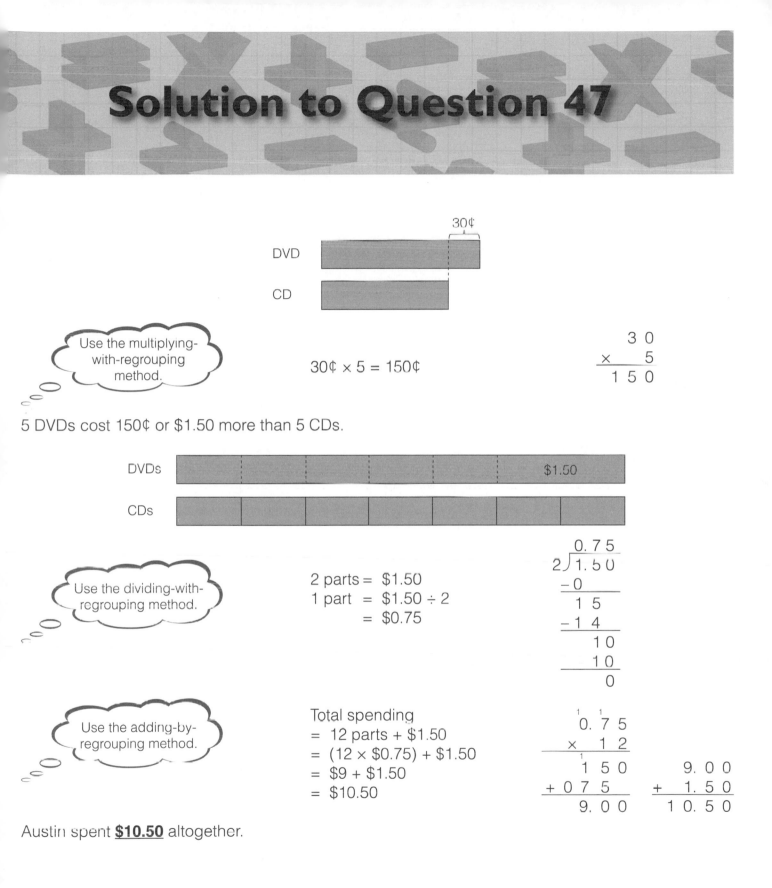

Use the multiplying-with-regrouping method.

$$30¢ \times 5 = 150¢$$

$$\begin{array}{r} 3\ 0 \\ \times\quad 5 \\ \hline 1\ 5\ 0 \end{array}$$

5 DVDs cost 150¢ or $1.50 more than 5 CDs.

DVDs $1.50

CDs

Use the dividing-with-regrouping method.

2 parts = $1.50
1 part = $1.50 ÷ 2
        = $0.75

$$\begin{array}{r} 0.7\ 5 \\ 2\overline{)1.5\ 0} \\ -0\quad \\ \hline 1\ 5\quad \\ -1\ 4\quad \\ \hline 1\ 0\ \\ 1\ 0\ \\ \hline 0\ \end{array}$$

Use the adding-by-regrouping method.

Total spending
= 12 parts + $1.50
= (12 × $0.75) + $1.50
= $9 + $1.50
= $10.50

$$\begin{array}{r} {}^{1}\ \ {}^{1}\ \ \\ 0.7\ 5 \\ \times\quad 1\ 2 \\ \hline {}^{1} \\ 1\ 5\ 0 \\ +\ 0\ 7\ 5 \\ \hline 9.0\ 0 \end{array}$$

$$\begin{array}{r} 9.0\ 0 \\ +\ 1.5\ 0 \\ \hline 1\ 0.5\ 0 \end{array}$$

Austin spent **$10.50** altogether.

Answer: **$10.50**

Use the guess-and-check method.

A cow has 4 legs.

A duck has 2 legs.

Number of cows	Number of legs	Number of ducks	Number of legs	Total number of animals	Total number of legs
7	7 × 4 = 28	7	7 × 2 = 14	14	28 + 14 = 42
8	8 × 4 = 32	6	6 × 2 = 12	14	32 + 12 = 44
6	**6 × 4 = 24**	**8**	**8 × 2 = 16**	**14**	**24 + 16 = 40**

There were **6** cows and **8** ducks.

Answer: **6 cows; 8 ducks**

Use the guess-and-check method.

Number of 50-dollar bills	Amount of money	Number of 20-dollar bills	Amount of money	Total number of bills	Total amount of money
5	5 × $50 = $250	5	5 × $20 = $100	5	$250 + $100 = $350
4	4 × $50 = $200	6	6 × $20 = $120	10	$200 + $120 = $320

He has **four** 50-dollar bills and **six** 20-dollar bills.

Answer: **Four 50-dollar bills; Six 20-dollar bills**

Use the guess-and-check method.

Number of 5-dollar bills	Amount of money	Number of 20-dollar bills	Amount of money	Total number of bills	Total amount of money
10	10 × $5 = $50	10	10 × $20 = $200	20	$50 + $200 = $250
11	11 × $5 = $55	9	9 × $20 = $180	20	$55 + $180 = $235
12	**12 × $5 = $60**	**8**	**8 × $20 = $160**	**20**	**$60 + $160 = $220**

There were **12** five-dollar bills and **8** twenty-dollar bills.

Answer: **12 five-dollar bills; 8 twenty-dollar bills**

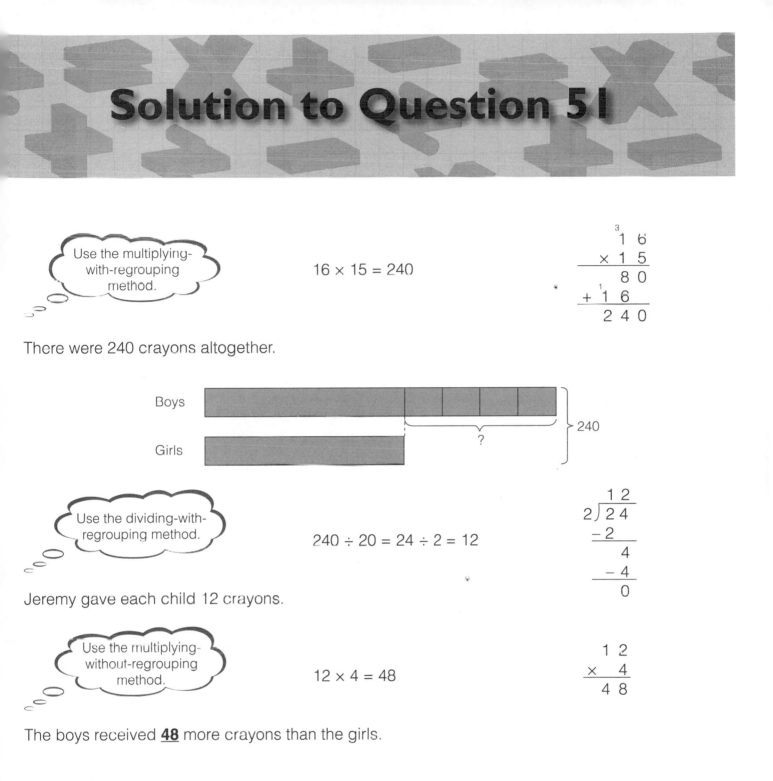

Use the multiplying-with-regrouping method.

$16 \times 15 = 240$

$$\begin{array}{r} \overset{3}{1}\,6 \\ \times\ 1\ 5 \\ \hline 8\ 0 \\ +\ \overset{1}{1}\ 6 \\ \hline 2\ 4\ 0 \end{array}$$

There were 240 crayons altogether.

Boys

Girls

240

?

Use the dividing-with-regrouping method.

$240 \div 20 = 24 \div 2 = 12$

$$\begin{array}{r} 1\ 2 \\ 2\overline{)2\ 4} \\ -2 \\ \hline 4 \\ -4 \\ \hline 0 \end{array}$$

Jeremy gave each child 12 crayons.

Use the multiplying-without-regrouping method.

$12 \times 4 = 48$

$$\begin{array}{r} 1\ 2 \\ \times\ \ 4 \\ \hline 4\ 8 \end{array}$$

The boys received **48** more crayons than the girls.

Answer: __48 more crayons__

A jacket = 2 parts

A pair of boots = 1 part

Therefore, each part is $35.

Use the multiplying-with-regrouping method.

$35 × 6 = $210

$$\begin{array}{r} \overset{3}{3}\,5 \\ \times \quad 6 \\ \hline 2\,1\,0 \end{array}$$

He had **$210** in the beginning.

Answer: _____ **$210**

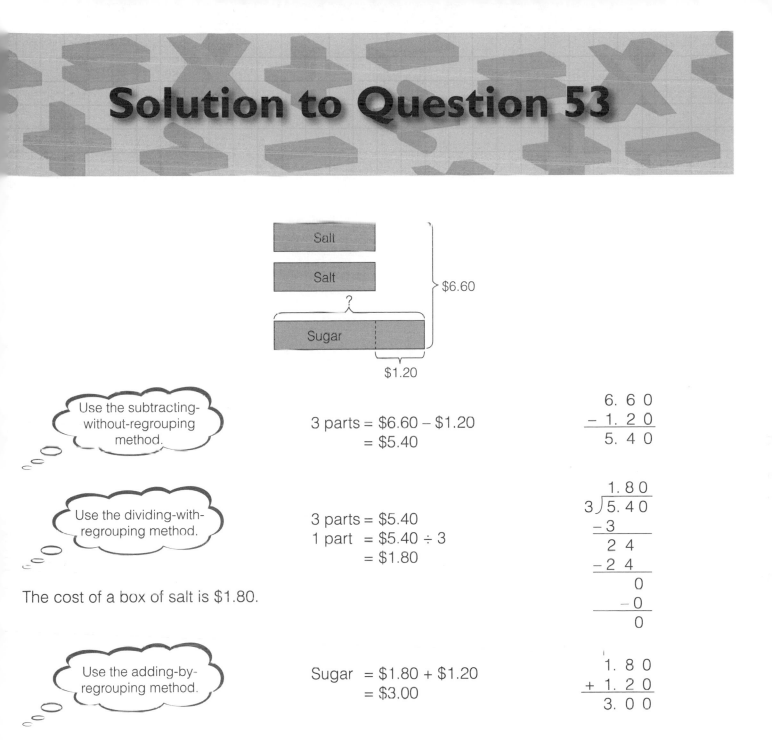

Use the subtracting-without-regrouping method.

3 parts = $6.60 – $1.20
= $5.40

$$\begin{array}{r} 6.\ 6\ 0 \\ -\ 1.\ 2\ 0 \\ \hline 5.\ 4\ 0 \end{array}$$

Use the dividing-with-regrouping method.

3 parts = $5.40
1 part = $5.40 ÷ 3
= $1.80

$$\begin{array}{r} 1.\,8\,0 \\ 3\overline{)5.\,4\,0} \\ -3 \\ \hline 2\,4 \\ -2\,4 \\ \hline 0 \\ -0 \\ \hline 0 \end{array}$$

The cost of a box of salt is $1.80.

Use the adding-by-regrouping method.

Sugar = $1.80 + $1.20
= $3.00

$$\begin{array}{r} 1.\ 8\ 0 \\ +\ 1.\ 2\ 0 \\ \hline 3.\ 0\ 0 \end{array}$$

The cost of a box of sugar is **$3**.

Answer: <u>   **$3**   </u>

Solution to Question 54

Use the multiplying-without-regrouping method.

$4 \times 5 = \$20$

5 mechanical pencils cost $20.

Use the subtracting-without-regrouping method.

$20 - \$10 = \$10$

Each pen cost $10.

$90 - \$20 = \$70$

June spent $70 on pens.

Use the dividing-without-regrouping method.

$70 \div \$10 = 7$

$10 \times 7 = 70$

She bought **7** pens.

Answer: ___**7 pens**___

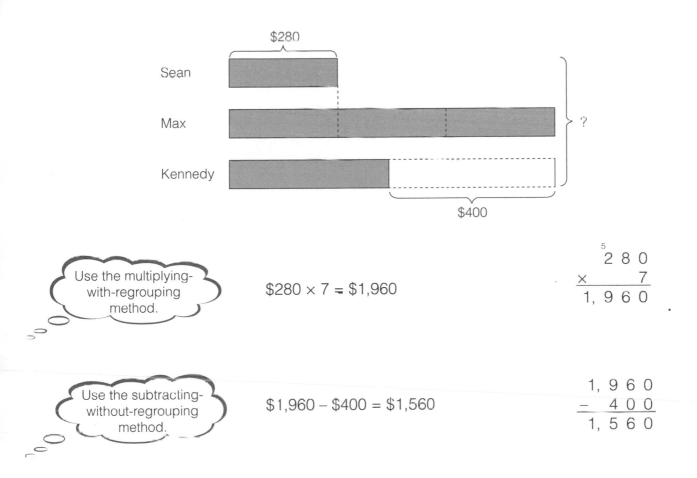

Use the multiplying-with-regrouping method.

$280 × 7 = $1,960

$$\begin{array}{r} \overset{5}{2}\,8\,0 \\ \times\quad\ 7 \\ \hline 1,9\,6\,0 \end{array}$$

Use the subtracting-without-regrouping method.

$1,960 − $400 = $1,560

$$\begin{array}{r} 1,9\,6\,0 \\ -\quad 4\,0\,0 \\ \hline 1,5\,6\,0 \end{array}$$

The total amount of money the 3 brothers received was **$1,560**.

Answer: __**$1,560**__

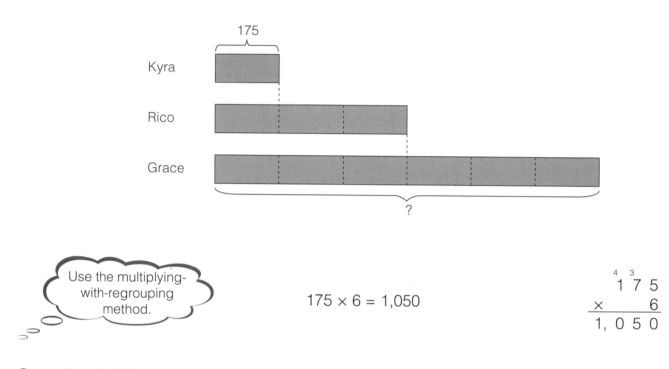

Use the multiplying-with-regrouping method.

$$175 \times 6 = 1,050$$

$$
\begin{array}{r}
{}^{4}\,{}^{3} \\
1\ 7\ 5 \\
\times\qquad 6 \\
\hline
1,\ 0\ 5\ 0
\end{array}
$$

Grace has **1,050** pieces of colored paper.

Answer: **1,050 pieces of colored paper**

$50 – $2.05

| Book | Book | Book | Book | Book | File | File | File | File | File | File | File | File | File |

$6.35

Use the subtracting-by-regrouping-twice method.

$50 – $2.05 = $47.95

$$\begin{array}{r} \overset{4}{\cancel{5}}\,\overset{9}{\cancel{0}}.\,\overset{9}{\cancel{0}}\,\overset{10}{\cancel{0}} \\ -\quad 2.\,0\,5 \\ \hline 4\,7.\,9\,5 \end{array}$$

5 books and 9 file folders cost $47.95.

Use the multiplying-with-regrouping method.

$6.35 × 5 = $31.75

$$\begin{array}{r} \overset{1}{}\,\overset{2}{} \\ 6.\,3\,5 \\ \times \quad\quad 5 \\ \hline 3\,1.\,7\,5 \end{array}$$

5 books cost $31.75.

Use the subtracting-without-regrouping method.

$47.95 – $31.75 = $16.20

$$\begin{array}{r} 4\,7.\,9\,5 \\ -\,3\,1.\,7\,5 \\ \hline 1\,6.\,2\,0 \end{array}$$

9 file folders cost $16.20.

Use the dividing-with-regrouping method.

$16.20 ÷ 9 = $1.80

$$\begin{array}{r} 1.\,8\,0 \\ 9\,\overline{)\,1\,6.\,2\,0} \\ -\,9 \\ \hline 7\,2 \\ -\,7\,2 \\ \hline 0 \\ -\,0 \\ \hline 0 \end{array}$$

Each file folder cost **$1.80**.

Answer: ___**$1.80**___

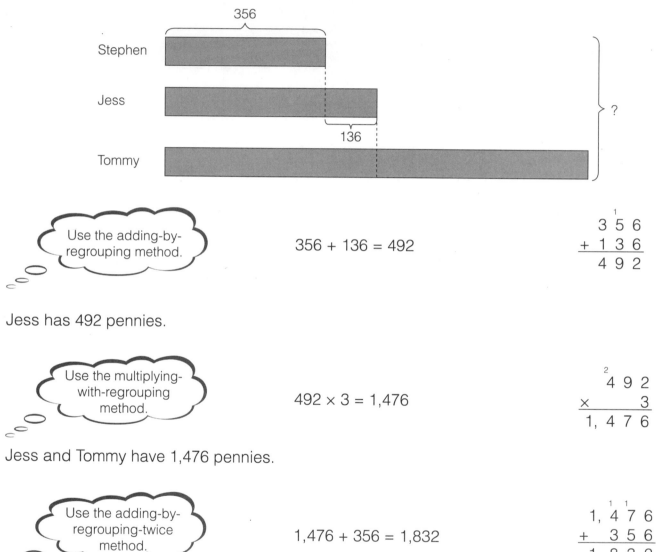

Stephen — 356

Jess

136

Tommy

?

> Use the adding-by-regrouping method.

$356 + 136 = 492$

$$\begin{array}{r} \overset{1}{3}\,5\,6 \\ +\ 1\,3\,6 \\ \hline 4\,9\,2 \end{array}$$

Jess has 492 pennies.

> Use the multiplying-with-regrouping method.

$492 \times 3 = 1,476$

$$\begin{array}{r} \overset{2}{4}\,9\,2 \\ \times\quad\ 3 \\ \hline 1,\ 4\,7\,6 \end{array}$$

Jess and Tommy have 1,476 pennies.

> Use the adding-by-regrouping-twice method.

$1,476 + 356 = 1,832$

$$\begin{array}{r} 1,\ \overset{1}{4}\,\overset{1}{7}\,6 \\ +\quad 3\,5\,6 \\ \hline 1,\ 8\,3\,2 \end{array}$$

They have **1,832** pennies altogether.

Answer: __1,832 pennies__

Solution to Question 59

Guess method

Using the lowest common multiple of 7 and 8,

Multiples of 7: 7, 14, 21, 28, 35, 42, 49, (56), 63, 70

Multiples of 8: 8, 16, 24, 32, 40, 48, (56), 64, 72, 80

$$56 + 5 = 61$$

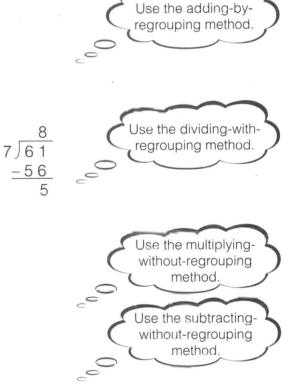

Use the adding-by-regrouping method.

Check method

If Mr. Knapp gave 8 children 7 stamps each,

$$61 \div 7 = 8 \text{ R } 5$$

$$\begin{array}{r} 8 \\ 7\overline{)61} \\ -56 \\ \hline 5 \end{array}$$

Use the dividing-with-regrouping method.

he would have 5 stamps left.

If Mr. Knapp gave 8 children 8 stamps each,

$$8 \times 8 = 64$$

$$64 - 61 = 3$$

Use the multiplying-without-regrouping method.

Use the subtracting-without-regrouping method.

he would need 3 more stamps.

Mr. Knapp had **61** stamps.

Answer: __**61 stamps**__

Solution to Question 60

Guess method

Using the lowest common multiple of 3 and 4,

Multiples of 3: 3, 6, 9, ⑫, 15, 18, 21, 24, 27, 30

Multiples of 4: 4, 8, ⑫, 16, 20, 24, 28, 32, 36, 40

$$12 + 2 = 14$$

Use the adding-without-regrouping method.

Check method

If Mrs. Reyes gave 4 students 3 apples each,

Use the dividing-with-regrouping method.

$$14 \div 3 = 4 \text{ R } 2$$

$$
\begin{array}{r}
4 \\
3{\overline{\smash{)}\,1\ 4}} \\
-1\ 2 \\
\hline
2
\end{array}
$$

she would have 2 apples left.

If Mrs. Reyes gave 4 students 4 apples each,

Use the subtracting-without-regrouping method.

$$4 \times 4 = 16$$

$$16 - 14 = 2$$

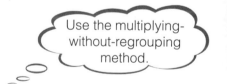
Use the multiplying-without-regrouping method.

she would need 2 more apples.

She had **14** apples.

Answer: ___**14 apples**___

(a)

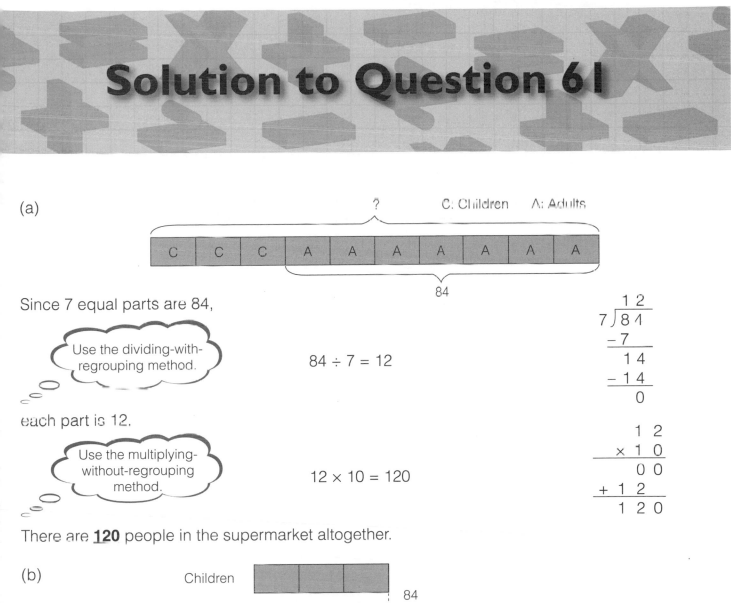

Since 7 equal parts are 84,

> Use the dividing-with-regrouping method.

$$84 \div 7 = 12$$

```
    1 2
7 ) 8 4
  - 7
    1 4
  - 1 4
      0
```

each part is 12.

> Use the multiplying-without-regrouping method.

$$12 \times 10 = 120$$

```
      1 2
  ×   1 0
      0 0
  + 1 2
  1 2 0
```

There are **120** people in the supermarket altogether.

(b)

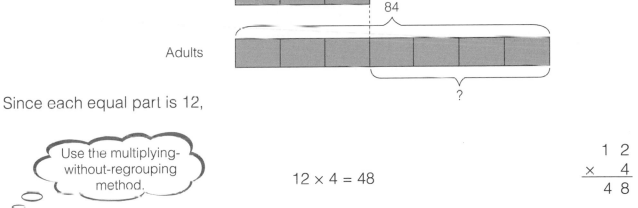

Since each equal part is 12,

> Use the multiplying-without-regrouping method.

$$12 \times 4 = 48$$

```
      1 2
  ×      4
      4 8
```

there are **48** more adults than children.

Answer: (a) __**120 people**__

(b) __**48 more adults**__

Solution to Question 62

(a)

Adults							

Children

800 ?

Since 5 equal parts are 800,

> Use the dividing-with-regrouping method.

$800 \div 5 = 160$

$$\begin{array}{r} 160 \\ 5\overline{)800} \\ -5 \\ \hline 30 \\ -30 \\ \hline 0 \\ -0 \\ \hline 0 \end{array}$$

each part is 160.

> Use the multiplying-with-regrouping method.

$11 \times 160 = 1,760$

$$\begin{array}{r} 160 \\ \times\ 11 \\ \hline 160 \\ +160 \\ \hline 1,760 \end{array}$$

There are **1,760** people at the concert hall altogether.

(b)
There are 480 children.

$160 \times 3 = 480$

$$\begin{array}{r} 1 \\ 160 \\ \times\ 3 \\ \hline 480 \end{array}$$

480

Girls	Girls	Girls	Boys	Boys	Boys	Boys	Boys

?

Since 8 equal parts are 480,

$480 \div 8 = 60$

$$\begin{array}{r} 60 \\ 8\overline{)480} \\ -48 \\ \hline 0 \\ -0 \\ \hline 0 \end{array}$$

each part is 60.

> Use the multiplying-without-regrouping method.

$2 \times 60 = 120$

$$\begin{array}{r} 60 \\ \times\ 2 \\ \hline 120 \end{array}$$

There are **120** more boys than girls.

Answer: (a) __1,760 people__

(b) __120 more boys__

Solution to Question 63

800

Novels   Nonfiction books

5 parts = 800
1 part = 800 ÷ 5
        = 160

2 parts = 160 × 2
        = 320

$$\begin{array}{r} 1\ 6\ 0 \\ 5\overline{)8\ 0\ 0} \\ -5 \\ \hline 3\ 0 \\ -3\ 0 \\ \hline 0 \\ -0 \\ \hline 0 \end{array}$$

$$\begin{array}{r} {}^1\ 1\ 6\ 0 \\ \times\ \ \ \ 2 \\ \hline 3\ 2\ 0 \end{array}$$

There were 320 novels.

800 − 320 = 480

$$\begin{array}{r} {}^7\ {}^{10} \\ 8\ \cancel{0}\ 0 \\ -3\ 2\ 0 \\ \hline 4\ 8\ 0 \end{array}$$

There were 480 nonfiction books.

For the novels,

320

Sold

8 parts = 320
1 part = 320 ÷ 8
        = 40

3 parts = 40 × 3
        = 120

$$\begin{array}{r} 4\ 0 \\ 8\overline{)3\ 2\ 0} \\ -3\ 2 \\ \hline 0 \\ -0 \\ \hline 0 \end{array}$$

$$\begin{array}{r} 4\ 0 \\ \times\ \ \ 3 \\ \hline 1\ 2\ 0 \end{array}$$

He sold 120 novels.

Thought bubbles: Use the dividing-with-regrouping method. Use the multiplying-with-regrouping method. Use the subtracting-with-regrouping method.

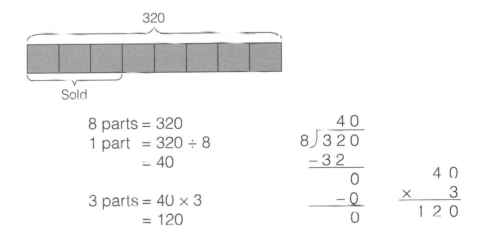

$$\$7 \times 120 = \$840$$

$$\begin{array}{r} \overset{1}{1}\,2\,0 \\ \times\quad 7 \\ \hline 8\,4\,0 \end{array}$$

He would make \$840 if he sold $\frac{3}{8}$ of the novels.

For the nonfiction books,

480

Sold

5 parts = 480
1 part = 480 ÷ 5
        = 96

2 parts = 96 × 2
        = 192

$$\begin{array}{r} 96 \\ 5\overline{)480} \\ -45 \\ \hline 30 \\ -30 \\ \hline 0 \end{array}$$

$$\begin{array}{r} \overset{1}{9}\,6 \\ \times\quad 2 \\ \hline 1\,9\,2 \end{array}$$

He sold 192 nonfiction books.

$$\$5 \times 192 = \$960$$

$$\begin{array}{r} \overset{4}{1}\,\overset{1}{9}\,2 \\ \times\quad 5 \\ \hline 9\,6\,0 \end{array}$$

He would make \$960 if he sold $\frac{2}{5}$ of the nonfiction books.

Use the adding-with-regrouping method.

$$\$840 + \$960 = \$1,800$$

$$\begin{array}{r} \overset{1}{8}\,4\,0 \\ +\quad 9\,6\,0 \\ \hline 1,\!8\,0\,0 \end{array}$$

He would make **\$1,800**.

Answer: ___**\$1,800**___

	?				
Mangoes	Sold	Sold			

Since 8 equal parts are 400,

Use the dividing-with-regrouping method.

$400 \div 8 = 50$

```
      50
  8)4 0 0
   -4 0
      0
     -0
      0
```

each part is 50.

Use the multiplying-without-regrouping method.

6000¢ = $60

$50 \times 2 = 100$

$100 \times 60¢ = 6,000¢$
$\qquad = \$60$

```
    5 0
  ×   2
  1 0 0
```

```
      1 0 0
    ×   6 0
      0 0 0
    + 6 0 0
    6, 0 0 0
```

Mr. Mead would make $60 if he sold $\frac{2}{3}$ of the mangoes.

$50 \times 4 = 200$

8000¢ = $80

$200 \times 40¢ = 8,000¢$
$\qquad = \$80$

```
    5 0
  ×   4
  2 0 0
```

```
      2 0 0
    ×   4 0
      0 0 0
    + 8 0 0
    8, 0 0 0
```

Mr. Mead would make $80 if he sold $\frac{4}{5}$ of the oranges.

Use the adding-by-regrouping method.

$\$60 + \$80 = \$140$

Mr. Mead would make **$140**.

Answer: _____**$140**_____

Convert $3\frac{1}{3}$ into a mixed fraction,

$$3\frac{1}{3} = \frac{10}{3}$$

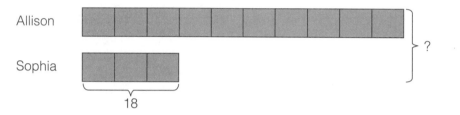

Allison

Sophia

?

18

Since 3 equal parts are 18,

$18 \div 3 = 6$

$6 \times 3 = 18$

each part is 6.

Use the multiplying-with-regrouping method.

$13 \times 6 = 78$

$$\begin{array}{r} \overset{1}{1}\,3 \\ \times\ \ 6 \\ \hline 7\,8 \end{array}$$

They have **78** stickers altogether.

Answer: __**78 stickers**__

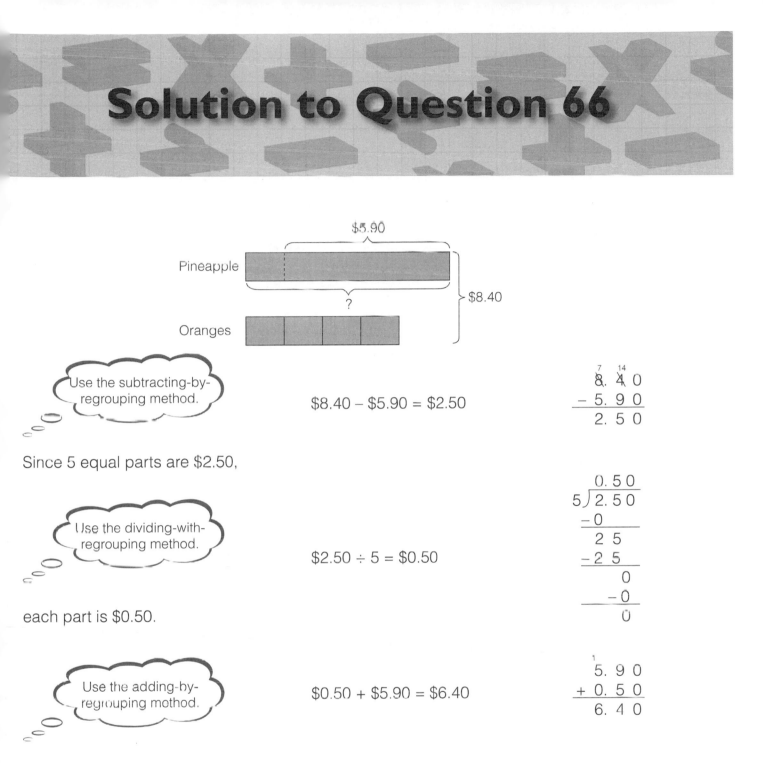

$8.40 - $5.90 = $2.50

Use the subtracting-by-regrouping method.

$$\begin{array}{r} ^7^{14} \\ 8.\ \cancel{4}\ 0 \\ -\ 5.\ 9\ 0 \\ \hline 2.\ 5\ 0 \end{array}$$

Since 5 equal parts are $2.50,

Use the dividing-with-regrouping method.

$2.50 ÷ 5 = $0.50

$$\begin{array}{r} 0.\ 5\ 0 \\ 5{\overline{\smash{\big)}\,2.\ 5\ 0}} \\ -0 \\ \hline 2\ 5 \\ -2\ 5 \\ \hline 0 \\ -0 \\ \hline 0 \end{array}$$

each part is $0.50.

Use the adding-by-regrouping method.

$0.50 + $5.90 = $6.40

$$\begin{array}{r} ^1 \\ 5.\ 9\ 0 \\ +\ 0.\ 5\ 0 \\ \hline 6.\ 4\ 0 \end{array}$$

The cost of the pineapple is **$6.40**.

Answer: **$6.40**

Solution to Question 67

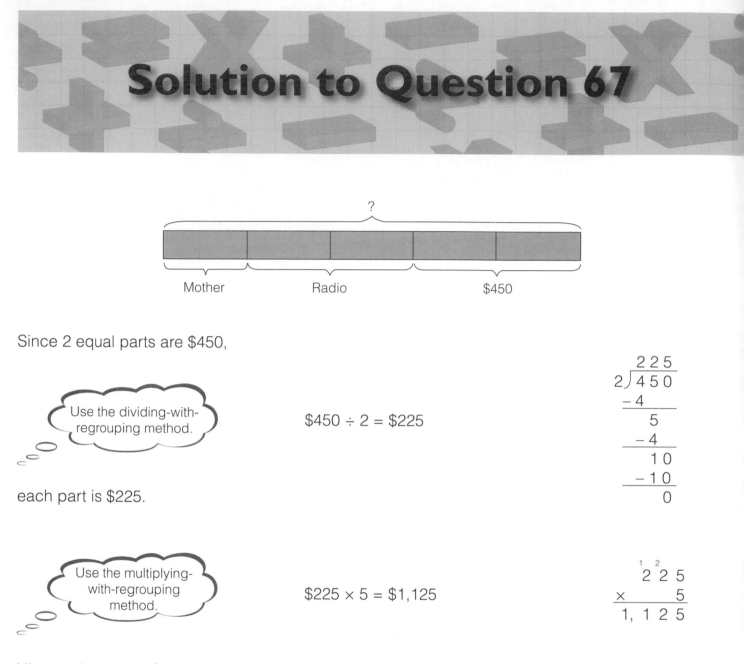

Since 2 equal parts are $450,

Use the dividing-with-regrouping method.

$450 ÷ 2 = $225

each part is $225.

$$\begin{array}{r} 225 \\ 2\overline{)450} \\ -4 \\ \hline 5 \\ -4 \\ \hline 10 \\ -10 \\ \hline 0 \end{array}$$

Use the multiplying-with-regrouping method.

$225 × 5 = $1,125

$$\begin{array}{r} {\scriptstyle 1\ 2} \\ 225 \\ \times\quad 5 \\ \hline 1,125 \end{array}$$

His paycheck was **$1,125**.

Answer: __**$1,125**__

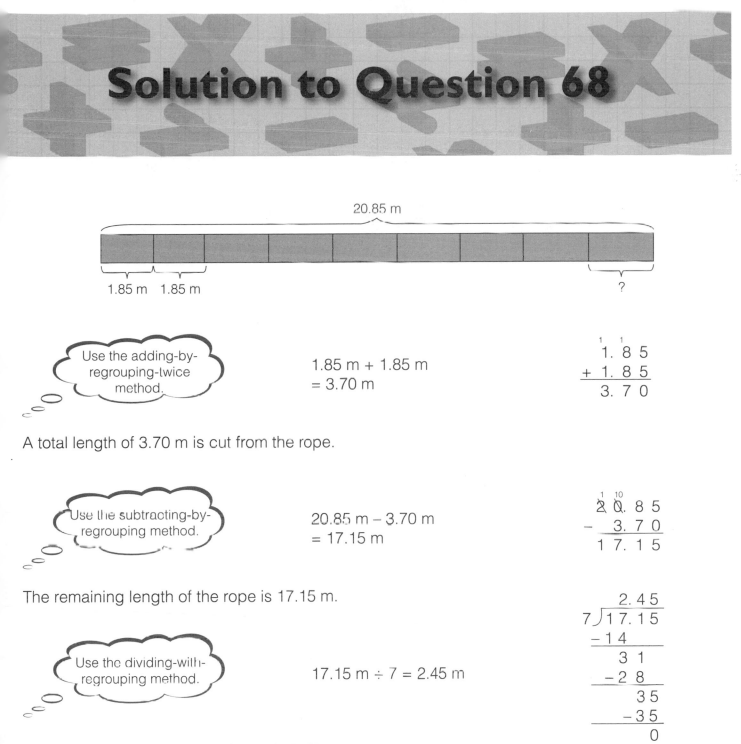

20.85 m

1.85 m   1.85 m   ?

Use the adding-by-regrouping-twice method.

1.85 m + 1.85 m
= 3.70 m

$$\begin{array}{r} \overset{1}{}\overset{1}{} \\ 1.\,8\,5 \\ +\;1.\,8\,5 \\ \hline 3.\,7\,0 \end{array}$$

A total length of 3.70 m is cut from the rope.

Use the subtracting-by-regrouping method.

20.85 m − 3.70 m
= 17.15 m

$$\begin{array}{r} \overset{1}{2}\,\overset{10}{0}.\,8\,5 \\ -\;\;3.\,7\,0 \\ \hline 1\,7.\,1\,5 \end{array}$$

The remaining length of the rope is 17.15 m.

Use the dividing-with-regrouping method.

17.15 m ÷ 7 = 2.45 m

$$\begin{array}{r} 2.\,4\,5 \\ 7\,\overline{)\,1\,7.\,1\,5} \\ -\,1\,4 \\ \hline 3\,1 \\ -\,2\,8 \\ \hline 3\,5 \\ -\,3\,5 \\ \hline 0 \end{array}$$

Each of the 7 equal pieces of rope is **2.45 m**.

Answer: _____**2.45 m**_____

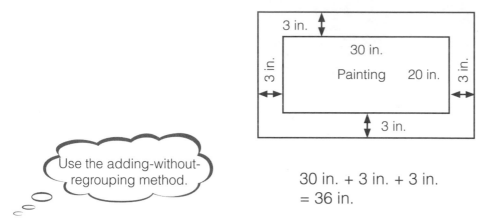

Use the adding-without-regrouping method.

30 in. + 3 in. + 3 in.
= 36 in.

The length of the painting with border is 36 in.

20 in. + 3 in. + 3 in. = 26 in.

The width of the painting with border is 26 in.

Use the multiplying-with-regrouping method.

36 in. × 26 in.
= 936 in.²

$$\begin{array}{r} {}^{1}{}_{3}\ \\ 3\ 6 \\ \times\ 2\ 6 \\ \hline 2\ 1\ 6 \\ +\ 7\ 2 \\ \hline 9\ 3\ 6 \end{array}$$

The area of the painting with border is 936 in.²

30 in. × 20 in. = 600 in.²

$$\begin{array}{r} 3\ 0 \\ \times\ 2\ 0 \\ \hline 0\ 0 \\ +\ 6\ 0 \\ \hline 6\ 0\ 0 \end{array}$$

The area of the painting is 600 in.²

Use the subtracting-without-regrouping method.

936 in.² − 600 in.²
= 336 in.²

$$\begin{array}{r} 9\ 3\ 6 \\ -\ 6\ 0\ 0 \\ \hline 3\ 3\ 6 \end{array}$$

The area of the border is **336 in.²**

Answer: _____**336 in.²**_____

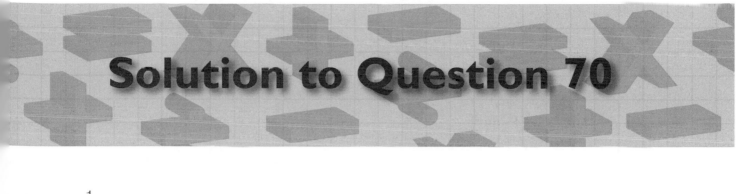

Change $\frac{1}{4}$ into an equivalent fraction.

$$\frac{1 \times 2}{4 \times 2} = \frac{2}{8}$$

Men	Men	Women	Women	Women	Women	Women	Children

?

100

Since 4 equal parts are 100,

Use the dividing-by-regrouping method.

$100 \div 4 = 25$

$$\begin{array}{r} 25 \\ 4\overline{)100} \\ -8 \\ \hline 20 \\ -20 \\ \hline 0 \end{array}$$

each part is 25.

Use the multiplying-with-regrouping method.

$8 \times 25 = 200$

$$\begin{array}{r} ^4 \\ 25 \\ \times8 \\ \hline 200 \end{array}$$

The total number of people in the theater was **200**.

Answer: **200 people**

Notes

Notes

Notes

Notes

Notes

Notes

Notes